I LOVE A SUNBURNT TORSO

and other country musings

BY THE SAME AUTHOR:
IT WASN'T MEANT TO BE EASY —
Tamie Fraser in Canberra.

I LOVE A SUNBURNT TORSO

and other country musings

CHRISTINA HINDHAUGH

Lothian Publishing Company
Melbourne · Sydney · Auckland

Produced by Ross Publishing

The author makes acknowledgement to *The Age, Farm Magazine*, the *West Australian* and *The Australian*, in whose pages have been published many of the articles which appear in this book.

First published 1987
by Lothian Publishing Company
Produced by Ross Publishing
Reprinted 1987, 1988

© Text: Christina Hindhaugh
© Illustrations: Mark Payne

Hindhaugh, Christina, 1944–
   I love a sunburnt torso, and other country musings.

   ISBN 0 85091 301 2.

   1. Country life — Australia — Anecdotes, facetiae, satire, etc. I. Title.

994

Designed by Sandra Nobes
Typeset by Bookset
Printed by Globe Press

For Christopher

CONTENTS

NANCY OF THE OVERTIME

I had written her a letter which I had, for want of better
　　Knowledge, sent to where I met her in a city office
　　clime;
A civil servant when I knew her, so I sent the letter to
　　her,
　　Just on spec, addressed as follows, 'Nancy of the
　　Overtime'.

And an answer came directed in a manner quite
　　expected,
　　(It was all computer printed, certainly not penned);
The staff department wrote it, and *verbatim* I will quote
　　it:
　　'Nancy's gone to Queensland flying; she's on a
　　long weekend.'

　　　　　. . .

In my wild erratic fancy visions come to me of Nancy
　　Working just nine days a fortnight, and making
　　heaps of dough;
In an office cool and gleaming with a staff to do the
　　cleaning,
　　For the city life has leisures that the rurals never
　　know.

And at lunch there's friends to meet her, and their
　　worldly voices greet her
　　In the murmur of the restaurant, where gourmet
　　food's the go,
And around the vision splendid of arcades and shops
　　extended,
　　And at night the wondrous glory of the concert
　　and the show.

　　　　　. . .

I am drenching in a rusty, stifling woolshed where a dusty
  Ray of sunlight sears fiercely down, like fire, on the wall:
And the foetid air impure from the piles of fresh manure
  Through the open battons wafting spreads its odour over all.

And in place of cultured chatter, I can hear the fiendish clatter
  Of the wethers and ewe weaners, as the sheep dogs give them chase;
And the language uninviting of my husband with them fighting
  Comes fitfully and loudly if I don't keep full the race.

And the hurrying hoggets haunt me, and their daggy backsides daunt me,
  As they poo on one another in their rush and nervous haste;
For I jostle and I push them; all day long I rush them,
  For a farmer has no time to rest, she has no time to waste.

And I sometimes rather fancy that I'd like to change with Nancy,
  Like to try some city living while I'm still within my prime;
While she faced the fight eternal with the dust and flies infernal—
  But I doubt she'd suit the sheepyards, Nancy of the Overtime.

With abject apologies
to A. B. Patterson

2

Job Specification

FARMER'S WIFE
(Grade 1)

DUTIES AND RESPONSIBILITIES: The successful applicant must be of sunny and gentle disposition, attractive in appearance, and capable of lifting a bag of wheat in one hand and two unshorn six-tooth wethers in the other. She must also be able to spend at least 14 hours a day on her feet, and remain patient and smiling—even when the blisters have burst.

The applicant must be an enthusiastic early riser, summer and winter, and possess an exceptional ability to organise her time. She will be expected to drench, draft and drove all day, come in at night and bath the kids, check the homework, feed the chooks, chop the wood, light the fire, take in the washing, do the ironing, cook the meal—and appear half an hour later for a little drink before dinner with her partner, looking like the front cover of Vogue.

Temperament is particularly important in this position and the applicant must possess the ability to remain calm and serene through flood, fire and footrot. She also needs the organisational ability to plan the family calendar each year. In this, sowing and harvest, hay-making and shearing are the main events. All other minor happenings like births, weddings, graduations and serious illnesses, etc. must be squeezed in between.

As well as proficiency in all areas of household management, some extra culinary skills are required for this position. These include an encyclopedic knowledge of how to make six-tooth appetising, month after month, plus the ability to rush in from the sheep yards at five to twelve and have a hot meal ready and steaming on the table by five past. As well, she needs special creative

3

powers to be able to produce a sumptuous repast out of absolutely nothing on those occasions when there are suddenly ten extra for dinner and the cupboard is bare.

The successful applicant in this position will find it necessary, because of time pressures, to undertake many different tasks concurrently. Thus she must possess enough motor skills and hand–eye co-ordination to be able to change a nappie, feed the pet lamb and whip up cake for the shearers—all at the same time. As well, cleanliness and neatness of workmanship are an advantage for use on those inevitable occasions when she will be required to change a tyre while wearing tennis clothes, push a car out of a bog in a dinner dress, or pull a calf in a nightie.

Special personnel management and human relationship skills are required in this position. The applicant will find herself responsible for the industrial harmony of the enterprise, and often will have to play a conciliation and arbitration role between her partner and his under-age staff when, for instance, those under-age staff have left the gate open between the bull paddock and the stud heifers—and mass retrenchments are threatened.

In the area of finance and cash-flow management, the applicant must accept that any spare income on a property will seldom be directed towards holidays or home-improvements, but rather towards keeping machinery manufacturers and chemical companies in business.

FORMAL QUALIFICATIONS: In order just to take up this position, the successful applicant must have a thorough working knowledge of carpentry, plumbing, mechanics, veterinary science, landscape gardening, interior decoration, hotel management, accountancy, law, medicine, psychology and diplomacy—just to name a few. Other necessary skills she will acquire on the job.

Applicants also need a fully-endorsed licence to drive a car, truck, tractor, motorbike, ride-on mower, pram and billy cart.

SALARY AND REMUNERATION PACKAGE:

Wages .... none
Overtime .... none
Weekend penalty rates .... none
Sickness benefits .... none
Holiday pay .... none
Long service leave .... none

FRINGE BENEFITS: Despite all, this position offers a lifestyle unique in opportunities for personal growth and fulfilment, freedom, and joy of living. In fact, most of its present incumbents would not swap it for the world!

THE A–Z OF COUNTRY LIVING

A city-dweller staying in the country once asked her host: 'What time do you leave for work in the mornings?' 'I don't,' replied the farmer. 'The minute I wake up I'm surrounded by it.'

This aspect of rural living (and a thousand others) makes country people different from city people. They have different attitudes, different customs—even a different vocabulary. This can cause problems when the two cultures meet.

In an attempt to obviate this communication gap, I have compiled a comprehensive *A–Z Guide to Country Life* so that city people can not only survive but also enjoy a weekend in the wilds with their rural rellies (the upmarket name for country cousins). If they study this list carefully and commit it to memory and/or their suitcase, they will never feel like Oscar Wilde who, when asked if he had been to the country recently, replied: 'Oh yes. I spent a month down there last weekend.'

A—ANIMALS: Principal inhabitants of farm who, it must be understood and accepted from the outset, will always take precedence over any visitor with the host for loving care and attention.

B—BULL: Male bovine variety of A. Also, how farmers regard comments or opinions tendered by city visitors in regard to the land—and almost anything else.

C—CALF, in: As in 'Lucy is in-calf': Stock adjectival phrase describing a cow or a woman who is *enceinte*.

D—DAGS: As in 'Rattle ya Dags!'; A country colloquialism meaning Hurry Up!

E—ESCAPEE: An A who breaks bounds. This always happens just before long-awaited outing or important dinner party, on a moonless night in a rainstorm.

F—FORWARD-STORE CONDITION: A rural expression for someone who has put on weight. 'You've been in a good paddock lately!' is another.

G—GATES: Obstructions between paddocks for visitors to grapple with in freezing wind. To avoid this ordeal, the quick-witted will always grab middle seat in paddock vehicle.

H—HAY: Small shards of dry grass, seeds and burrs used as decorative attachments to socks and sweaters.

I—IDLENESS: A foreign word like 'holidays', not known to farmers but often dreamed about longingly in secret by their wives.

J—JOIN, to: A rural expression for procreating. Hence in the country the expression: 'May I join you?' can bring thoroughly delightful but totally unforeseen consequences.

K—KITCHEN GARDEN: Large and forbidding area of vegetables cultivated by farmer's wife and usually plundered at the height of its production by heavy-footed E's.

L—LUNCHTIME: That time of day when stock agents, sales reps or loads of fertiliser arrive.

M—MANURE: Foul-smelling viscose substance with an irresistible attraction to toddlers not yet steady on their feet.

N—NUTS AND BOLTS: Small pieces of discarded metal which lie around the house on windowsills and mantlepieces for months until finally thrown out in exasperation by farmer's wife, whereupon instantly they become essential and irreplaceable.

O—OFF, as in 'Getting it off!': In the country this is not an inelegant expression of sexual achievement, but merely refers to harvesting the crop.

P—PARTY (usually dinner): Prevalent form of rural

social intercourse where the men gather around the bar to discuss the weather/worms/weaners and the women gather around the fire to discuss the men.

Q—QUIT: What a farmer's wife threatens to do everytime the E's plunder her K.

R—RIPPED OFF: What a farmer considers is happening to his industry in Australia today when he must buy his inputs on a closed market, sell his products on an open market, and pay the freight both ways.

S—SEPTIC TANK: Farm sewerage disposal apparatus which works perfectly unless there are visitors in the house.

T—TELEPHONE: Small, but persistent, talking machine similar to its city counterpart but with its bell mechanism curiously linked to meal times.

U—UNWARY: Visitors who think they have been asked to stay purely for the pleasure of their company. See V.

V—VISITORS: Source of cheap labour.

W—WEATHER: Universal rural obsession and principal topic of conversation. Hence remarks like: 'It's on the way down' or 'It's steady' refer not to a lift, interest rates or the CPI, but the barometer.

X—XMAS: Christian gift-giving festival held in the middle of harvest of sufficient importance for farmer to take two hours off his tractor for roast turkey dinner.

Y—YEAR, next: That time when a farmer is definitely going to buy his wife a promised dishwasher/drier/TV etc.

Z—Zzzzzzzz: The only conversation of which the city visitor is capable after the exertion, the exhaustion—and the exhilaration—of a country weekend!

P.S.T.

Although our city friends may be prone to such urban afflictions as lung pollution, executive burn-out or strap-hanger's elbow, at least they never have to suffer that peculiarly country complaint known as Pre-Shearing Tension.

PST is a strange neuro-physiological disorder which strikes a farmer just before shearing time and transforms even the gentlest of souls into a wild-eyed tyrant.

The condition is not new. Indeed, oral evidence suggests it has been chronic and endemic amongst farming families for generations. Luckily it is only a temporary, seasonal derangement, but while it lasts it causes strange personality disorders and paranoid behaviour patterns which can upset a farmer's entire central nervous system—or family, as it is often called.

I have spent the last 18 shearing seasons in silent observation and awed analysis of this malaise, yet in all those years I have never heard of it being medically recognised nor clinically defined.

But from my research, the symptoms are these: about a week to 10 days before his sheep are due to be shorn, the sufferer's (the farmer's) blood pressure soars, his tolerance level plunges, his eyes become glassy and distracted and his mind obsessed with irrational fears.

This is the time for all sufferees (his partner, small children, dogs and in-laws) to tread very softly and generally Keep Out Of The Way.

His irrational fears will include an unshakeable conviction that the wool-classer will not turn up, the shearers will go on strike, the overhead gear seize, the battens collapse, the yards flood and the weaners suddenly sprout dags the size of avocados—and have to be re-crutched.

All four sheep dogs will be run over, the motorbike

9

break down, the wool press break up and flystrike break out.

If a sufferee sweetly and gently points out that none of these disasters has ever happened before and anyway he would cope and anyway why not relax and take it easy and try not to worry, she will receive such rejoiners as: 'But I'm *not* worrying!' or 'I'm perfectly *calm*, thank you! ! !' or 'I *know there's no need to shout!*'

This is a critical stage of the illness and any small sufferee who dares smile, let alone laugh aloud, is liable to a quick clip over the ear—known at this time of the year as a Wool Clip.

I regret to say I know of no antidote for this affliction. The only treatment seems to be to ignore the symptoms, remain patient and serene, and Carry On No Matter What. But I always take care to ensure that no unnecessary handles are left lying around the house for the sufferer to fly off, and though he may have trouble sleeping at night, I've found it unwise in the extreme to suggest counting sheep.

Luckily, the condition doesn't last long and recovery is usually rapid and complete. When the last sheep is shorn on the last day of shearing, Mr Hyde disappears and lovely Dr Jekyll returns once more.

Perhaps there are some city equivalents to PST? Maybe retailers suffer from Pre-Stocktaking Sale Tension, factory managers become afflicted with Pre-Production Deadline Tension and executive directors struck down by Pre-Shareholders' Annual General Meeting Tension? If so, I suspect the symptoms—and the treatment—are the same.

Last year after a certain farmer I know, but who shall remain nameless for ethical reasons, had just emerged from a particularly severe bout of PST, I remarked: 'Darling, it's incredible. You were a completely different person last week than you are for the rest of the year. I think perhaps you're schizophrenic.'

He gave me a wicked smile, and said: 'You know, I've half a mind to agree!'

A HEADY AFFAIR

Heartbreak Hotel,
Balmoral.

Dear Dorothy Dix,

Please can you help me? My husband is having an affair with *a header*!

As you know, he's been dreaming about owning his own header for years. Well, last week he finally succumbed to temptation and went out and bought one. And now his passion for this Iron Lady makes Abelard's love for Heloise seem like an off-hand affair.

Dorothy, what can I do? The humiliating part is she's *not even young*! Worn, chipped, positively rusting in parts, he found her sitting in a second-hand machinery yard in a small town about 100 k's from here—and it was love at first sight. Quite undaunted by her lack of cabin or air conditioning, he simply erected a beach umbrella over the operator's seat and drove her all the way home on a day at least 40 degrees in the waterbag, arriving about sunset puce in the face, covered with dust, and smiling as though all his Christmases had come at once.

Since then I've hardly seen him. He spends every waking hour down in the machinery shed attending to his new love, servicing her moving parts, checking her open front, and doing exactly *what* to her *seed box* I scarcely dare imagine.

Today was the day to begin stripping the crop. Miss Steel (as he calls her) was ready—tuned, oiled and polished to within an inch of her life. Changing through the gears with great tenderness, he drove her out to the paddock while I followed along behind in the ute with the fuel and spares, seething.

The day was hot and still and the wheat shimmered like gold in the sun. As he manoeuvred her over to the edge of the crop Miss Steel bellowed her excitement, emitting hot blasts of black smoke.

When they reached the edge of the crop they halted for a moment and he revved her engine several times, testing the controls. Then, when he had her coaxed to a state of roaring, shuddering readiness he left in the clutch—and they took off down the row together in mutual ecstasy and a cloud of dust. I went straight home and had a cold shower.

I suppose I should have known it would happen one day. You see he's had some minor *affairs de coeur* before. He was pretty keen on a New Holland Big Baler at one stage, but a couple of broken chains and a jammed intake at the height of the hay-making season soon snapped him out of that. On another occasion he had a mild flirtation with a new Hardi Boom Spray, but continually blocked nozzles soon cooled his ardour there.

Perhaps the most serious case up until now was a prolonged and rather stormy infatuation with his spring-release rigid-tyne drill. That affair ran hot and cold for ages, but last year when direct drilling a new paddock a submerged rock broke the under-carriage—and the spell—and that was the end of that.

But all those affairs were but mere flirtations compared with the *grande passion* he holds for Miss Steel!

So, Dorothy, what can I do? If my rival were but Another Woman, I could fight back! Dye my hair! Lose some weight! Change my wardrobe! But how can I compete with a Massey Ferguson 585?

Please send me your advice as soon as possible.

I am strongly contemplating *sabotage*.

Yours, etc.

Desperate,
Balmoral. Vic.

NOW I LAY ME DOWN TO SLEEP . . .

There is an Egyptian axiom: 'The worst thing is to be in bed, and sleep not.' I agreed.

The other night I lay awake for hours tossing and turning and trying desperately to will myself into the Land of Nod. But it was no use. At the very witching time of night the churchyards might well have been yawning—but I was wide awake.

Why is Morpheus so fickle, I wondered as I lay there in the dark? Why is it that only two hours ago when seated on hard chairs in a cavernous and freezing country hall I could not keep my eyes open, yet now in the warmth and comfort of my bed I feel totally alert?

I had been attending a meeting, and at the point on the agenda where I was to deliver my Hon. Treasurer's report all the audience heard from me was a gentle snore. The junior vice-president, a true friend, surreptitiously kicked me in the shins and I leapt to my feet and began reading out the list of figures from a piece of paper I had grabbed from my pocket as I stood up.

Halfway through I realised that these figures were not the profit-and-loss account at all, but last week's Tattslotto results. The ensuing uproar guaranteed that when I returned home and went to bed there was no way I could relax and drop off to sleep.

Mind you, I did try. First I began with the age-old remedy, counting sheep. Two, four, six,—I watched the sheep closely as they ran past my mind's eye— eight, ten (needs crutching), 12, (should be drenched), 14, 16—fly strike on 16! Stop the mob! It is not a soporific experience for a country person to count sheep.

Next I tried lists. A friend once told me that on sleepless nights she goes through the books of the Bible: Genesis, Exodus, Leviticus, etc. She says drowsiness

13

sets in about Chronicles I or II and she usually drops off about Ezekiel, although on a bad night she may have to go as far as Zachariah. I know other people who list VFL premiership teams, or winners of the Melbourne Cup.

But when I tried these remedies they came out as Genesis, Exodus, Collingwood, At Talaq . . . and had not the slightest somnolent effect. Neither had the next lists I silently recounted: the Great Kings of England, from William the Conqueror through to George VI; nor the Great Queens of England from Oscar Wilde through to Quentin Crisp!

Maybe somehow I had frighted gentle sleep, nature's soft nurse, like Henry IV, who had the most famous wakeful night in literature. But Henry's sleeplessness was due to anxiety over a battle he faced on the morrow, whereas I had no impending battle to keep me awake, except with my daughter over wearing thongs to the school social. Come to think of it, my battle may well be the harder to win . . .

My husband has a fail-safe way of getting to sleep. On those nights when he feels restless and wakeful he asks me to go through all the jobs which I have been waiting (and waiting and waiting) for him to do around the house: 'One, fix the dripping tap in the shower; two, unblock the outside gully trap; three, mend the broken pane in the garage window; four . . . ' well, he has never yet lasted past three before being overtaken by deep and blissful slumber.

But I do not think the technique would work for me. If he started saying: 'one, replace the button on my white shirt; two, weed the carrot patch; three, sponge the spots on the hall carpet,' I probably would become so stricken with guilt that I would leap out of bed then and there and start in on them.

Is there a special technique in willing yourself to sleep, I pondered, as I lay there in the darkness, listening to the hall clock strike yet again? I mean, if Rip van Winkle can fall asleep for 20 years in a mountain cave, Epimenides for 57 years in a Cretan cave, and Sleeping Beauty for 100 years in an enchanted castle, surely here, safely tucked up in my own bed, I . . .

14

TIME AND MANAGEMENT

If you come up behind a muddy ute on the highway one day which is weaving all over the road, don't worry. Chances are the driver is not drunk, high on drugs or having a heart attack. He's just a farmer busily absorbed in managing all his neighbours' properties.

It never ceases to amaze me how farmers, always over-worked and under stress on their own places, still feel the need to manage everyone else's? It's a compulsion. An obsession.

Every time my husband drives to town, all along the way he carefully checks up on whatever his neighbours are doing.

'Oh, look. Stan's shifted his weaners into a fresh paddock.' he says, jabbing his finger at the ute window and pointing somewhere off into the middle distance. 'That's good. They should pick up there. But he'll have to watch for staggers in that ryegrass.'

'Ah, yes. I see Bill's spray-topped a pasture. That should help the clover get away. I wonder what rate of chemical he used? But look! His lambs have started scouring. I hope he's drenched them.'

Meanwhile, the ute is going all over the road and a car behind has been trying to pass for four miles.

'Oh, no! Look at the dock in that wheat crop!' he exclaims further on, to be honest, more with relish than with sympathy. 'Should have used a herbicide. He cropped that paddock in wheat last year, too, I remember. Hope he's sown with a fungicide-amended fertiliser otherwise he'll have take-all as well. And *when* is he going to doze out those stumps?'

Let me emphasise that this dedicated roadside management does not occur merely within our own district, where perhaps some degree of local knowledge and expertise could be claimed. Oh no. My husband is perfectly at ease managing estates all the way to Melbourne, 400 k's away.

'I wonder what he's sown there?' he'll say, gazing over a fence as we weave down the highway. Sometimes his curiosity becomes too much to bear and he'll stop the car, leap out and hop over the fence for a look. And if, by any chance, there's some poor unsuspecting farmer pulled up in a paddock by the side of the road to re-fuel or service his equipment, my husband pounces on him with a stream of questions, and I'm lucky if I get to Melbourne by the following day.

Still, at least he is quite unbiased about it, and manages each property individually, solely on its own merits. A friend of mine told me that when her husband is roadside managing he always compares every aspect of each property with his own back home—and all *favourably*. 'Oh, look, will you? His weaners are much bigger than ours. Probably cut heavier, too. Mind you, he has much more feed. It doesn't get nearly so cold and wet in winter down here, either. If only my cattle looked like that! They're probably quieter and easier to handle than ours, too. That crop looks heavy. I wonder what it'll yield? But then, this country's so much better drained.'

By the time she reaches town, she's almost in tears.

For me, the one disappointing aspect of this roadside management is that none of my husband's clients has ever yet offered to pay for his services. All his briefs are entirely honorary and unsolicited, rendered only from the goodness of his heart. But more than once has the thought occurred to me that if only we could collect consulting fees from all those properties, we'd be rich beyond our wildest dreams.

And, believe me, we have some pretty wild dreams.

One thing does faintly worry me in all this, however. Returning home from town last week I happened to notice some weaving tyre-tracks meandering along the road beside our fenceline, and the question suddenly struck me that while we are busily occupied managing everyone else's property—I wonder just *who* out there is managing ours?

A CAMERA NEVER LIES

Primitive tribes believe that if someone takes their photograph, they lose their soul. With a driver's licence photograph, that is true.

I have just had my photograph taken by the Road Traffic Authority as now required by the law in this state. I found the experience debilitating and the result appalling. Frankly, if I really looked the way I appear, I would be far too ill to drive.

My photograph was especially disappointing as I had made such an effort to achieve a pleasing result. On the appointed day I went to the RTA office dressed to kill; hair freshly blow-waved, make-up immaculate, nails carefully manicured.

'Why the big deal?' asked the family, highly amused. 'It's only for your driver's licence, you know, not the front cover of Vogue!' But as I told them, *any* photograph is important to a woman over 40. Besides, I said, I will be required to flash it at strange policemen all over the country; it is only natural I should wish to look my best. 'But why paint your fingernails?' cried the family in hysterics. 'They won't show!' 'I know,' I answered them huffily, 'but if a woman's hands say housework it shows on her face.'

The RTA office was a cluster of tin sheds situated on the outskirts of our local provincial city, and instead of a spacious studio, I was shown into a tiny booth.

'Stand right there, thank you madam,' said the fresh-faced attendant, pointing to a mark on the floor against the wall. 'This will only take a minute.' She peered into the lens of her giant camera which stood threateningly at eye level in front of me, its four legs splayed out.

'Just keep quite still and look pleasant until you hear the camera click,' she said. 'Then you can relax.' Just what did she mean by that, I wondered?

But this was no time for reflection, I had to concentrate. Pleasant, she had said. But how does one look Pleasant? Pleasant is not an expression I can consciously put on. I can do Happy or Sad and I have Astonished, Exasperated or Furious at will. So has anyone who is married. But Pleasant is not in my repertoire.

Anyway, I thought wistfully, has age and motherhood reduced me to merely Pleasant? My mind went back to teenage years and the hours spent practising useful looks in front of a mirror. My favourites were Pale, Frail and Interesting, and Daring, Dramatic and Dangerous-to-Know. These I had perfected at 13 but had never used since, except sometimes at parent/teacher interviews. They might come in handy now.

'Right!' said the attendant. 'All set. But madam, why are you leaning forward like that?'

'Because it hides my double chin,' I replied smiling, supremely confident she instantly would deny its existence. Instead she said: 'But that is a distinctive feature. I need to highlight your distinctive features in a licence photo.'

'What about the distinctive line of my Garbo brow or the distinctive curve of my Susan Hampshire nose?' I asked.

'No, but there is a chicken pox scar under your, right nostril which shows up rather well, and on your left cheek there is a nice big mole.'

'That's not a mole! It's a Beauty Spot!' I thundered, and glared at her in outrage. Click, went the camera.

In the mail three weeks later I received the result securely attached to my driver's licence. My hair was a horse's mane after it has rolled in a well-used sheep camp; my features were a granite rock on a frosty morning; my eyes had the animation of an overfat ewe in a dust storm.

'Never mind, Mum,' said my daughter, when I finally revealed it to the family. 'Shirley Temple used to have her photograph taken through gauze. Next time I'll make sure you have some linoleum.'

AN AVID AVANT GARDENER

High spring is here! Gardens all around the district are ablaze with colour and exuberance! It's the season when, as Ralph Waldo Emerson once said, 'the earth laughs with flowers'.

Until a few years ago I only knew three kinds of flowers: wild, tame and cauli. You see, I've come only recently to a love of gardening. I suppose you could call me an Avant Gardener.

Nowadays my garden is my closest friend. Ours is a symbiotic relationship. I tend to its physical needs and it tends to my spiritual needs. For what greater healing for the mind can there be to sit in the garden, silent and alone, and listen to the flowers grow?

But I have not always felt this way. In the past I regarded my garden as The Enemy. It threatened all my idle hours. It oppressed and haunted me. For how, having finally reached the bottom of the ironing basket and the mending pile, could I possibly without conscience grab five minutes to sit and read, when always, always the garden was out there waiting for attention?

Periodically its wild vigour forced me into frantic bursts of disciplinary action with secateurs and spade—but for the rest of the year I treated it with malevolent neglect.

Then, a few weeks after our youngest child went off to school, I happened to look out the front window one morning and to my astonishment saw, not the usual threatening tangle of botanical aggression, but—wonder of wonders—a beautiful latent garden crying to be freed!

I felt like Saul on the road from Tarsus.

Tingling with excitement, I grabbed the nearest pair of gumbies, brushed the rust off the fork and hoe,

19

shook the spiders out of the canvas gloves, and dashed off out into the sunshine to become—a born-again gardener.

Now what is a gardener? How is she different from other people? (I say 'she' because around these parts most gardeners are women. With some notable exceptions, the term 'plant husbandry' is a misnomer.)

From my observations, a gardener is someone whose pockets are always stuffed with miscellaneous seeds and pods. She is the one whose handbag bulges with bulbs and corms and whose basket drips with cuttings and roots.

A gardener is someone who cannot pass a cowpat without picking it up, cannot notice a weed without pulling it out and cannot spy and deadhead without snapping it off. She has knees tough as tanbark, hands rough as pine cones, and though she may weep at a rain-damaged bloom, she can squash a live snail without flinching.

As well, a gardener is a relentless optimist who cheerfully disregards all the accepted laws of physics. She bases her life work on the premise that what goes down must come up.

But, strangely enough, a gardener is also the person in all the world least likely to lead you up the garden path. As Rolande Browne once wrote: 'I don't know whether it is that nice people grow roses, or whether growing roses makes people nicer.'

Now, to be honest, what I still grow mostly in my garden is *tired*. I have a long way to go before I'm a real, live state-of-the-art gardener. I'm not yet even a common or garden gardener.

But I am an avant gardener, and thus have all the passion and reckless enthusiasm of the newly converted. I have become familiar with two more varieties of flowers (plain and self-raising) and I now know that a garden is a thing of beauty and a job forever.

PERCENTAGE LIVING

There are only two kinds of statistics—the kind you look up and the kind you make up. Both kinds are flourishing today.

Life has become saturated with statistics. After the $ sign, surely the % sign is the most used (and abused) symbol of the modern world? I mean, you rise in the morning to breakfast upon 36% natural fibre cereal, 70% pure orange juice and 12% starch-reduced toast. You go out on the farm to mark 98% lambs from ewes which are growing 3% more wool at a 12% increased stocking rate with 7% less supplementary feeding but a 30% increased drenching program. You handle 24% more sheep per hour with 52% less outside labour and therefore run 25% behind 95% of the time.

Back in the office you are faced with a 20% prime interest rate, 10% inflation, 0.001% return on capital, 25% increase in costs and 38% reduction in returns.

Of course figures cannot lie—except when liars figure—and it is gloriously easy to prove anything with statistics: that umbrellas cause rain, that bikinis cause suntan and that accidents cause people.

The advertising industry is probably the most unethical user of statistics. 'This shampoo makes your hair 14% cleaner and 19% easier to manage!' What they never mention is *than what?* Washing it in creosote and sump oil? 'These cigarettes are 10% smoother and 17% more satisfying!' *Than what?* Saw dust wrapped in gum leaves?

Lately I have noticed a trend for advertisers to use fractional percentages, I suppose to keep pace with the increasing levels of education and expertise in the community. Thus Sheep Drench A does not kill 18% more internal parasites than Sheep Drench B, but 18.5/8% more. Chemical X broadleaf herbicide is not 23% more effective than Chemical Y, but 23 7/9% more effective.

Retail stores are lavish and sometimes unprincipled users of percentages. They know an inveterate bargain-hunter like me finds a '30% OFF!!' sign or a '50% SALE!!' sign totally irresistible, even though I am fully aware the 30% usually means the item is now priced at 30% less than twice its normal price, and a 50% sale probably only means there is 50% more stock in the shop at the time.

Small wonder then that I was caught out so easily when I bought a clock for the woolshed in a '25% OFF!!' sale at a country store. On taking the 'bargain' proudly home, I discovered it lost 15 minutes every hour. 'Didn't you see the '25% OFF' sign?' asked the store-keeper when I took the clock back to complain. 'That referred to the time mechanism, not the price!'

Statistical measurements have now intruded into every aspect of farm life. Stocking rates, wool production, pasture growth, crop yields, weight gains, time management and personal productivity all are now chartered in constant comparative ratios.

I suppose it won't be long before percentage measurements will be introduced into personal relationships as well. 'Darling, I find you 74% caring and 82% supportive, and I'm glad to say your tenderness quotient is up 5% from last week's low of 48%.

Even day-to-day grievances may soon be quantified as well. 'This week you've spent 17% less time in the sheep yards and 32% more on the golf course!' or 'There's still 36 2/5% more digging to be done in the vege. garden and 86% more manure needed from under the shed!' or 'Watchout! I'm 100% fed up!'

That percentages have run amok was finally brought home to me on reading a newspaper clipping pinned to a woolshed wall, saying: 'The first 90% of the job takes 90% of the time, and the last 10% takes the other 90%.'

OUT OF THE MOUTHS OF BABES . . .

Of all the great and enlightened educational innovations introduced into our schools in recent times, the one I like least is Show and Tell.

Show and Tell is where young children address their peers in class for a few minutes each morning to describe the highlights of their daily lives.

The educational theory behind it is supposed to be the development of self-confidence, oral fluency, clarity of expression, etc. But I know better. Show and Tell is an invidious plot on behalf of teachers to find out What Goes On At Home.

'Good morning, boys and girls. Did you have a nice day?' asks the teacher each morning—and by recess there is nothing that's happened in the entire district which she doesn't know about.

Who went where for dinner. Who has what illness. Who lost at the races. Who has a new car/boat/video. Who skipped church for golf. It's not so much Show and Tell as Days of Our Lives.

'My Dad went to town for the weekend so Mr Stanley from next door came over to look after Mum and see she wasn't lonely. He comes over whenever Dad's away.'

'My Dad says old Len Stokes down the road claims his grog as a tax deduction. He puts it down as drench. But Mum says that's okay, because for him it is drench.'

'My Dad's thrilled with his new rifle, and I reckon he must be the best shot in the district. He says he hasn't missed a sheep yet.'

'Mum bogged the ute in the back paddock and had to walk home.'

'Dad's got itch-mite in the weaners.'

'My sister's been away for a little operation.'

'If anyone wants a video, my big brother's got a couple going cheap.'

Of course there is no greater exponent of the narrative art than a child with a captive audience, and these daily reports of life at home lose nothing in the telling. Recently I heard from another child in the same class that my daughter had announced in Show and Tell one morning that 'when there's no-one around at home, my Mummy dresses up in my Dad's clothes.' Now can't you imagine that little pearly gem going straight back to the staff room at morning tea?

Such was my embarrassment over this disclosure that I avoided both the teacher and the school for as long as possible, but confrontation was inevitable and my moment of truth came when I was summoned for the annual parent/teacher interview.

As I sat before the teacher and was regaled with my child's performance in number facts and language areas, I found it impossible to concentrate on what she was saying. Should I explain that the incident which prompted my daughter's remarks was merely me choosing some dress-up clothes for a Brideshead Revisited party where I was to appear as Sebastian (my husban was Charles—we made a striking couple) and that actually I do *not* have transvestite tendencies?

Or should I ignore the matter and leave well enough alone?

As it turned out, sheer lack of nerve made me choose the latter option, but I was never again able to look that teacher squarely in the eye.

However, I believe teachers should know that they don't have everything all their own way. We parents have a great defence. You see, we hear some pretty funny things about them, too.

Our children come home with some very peculiar stories sometimes about What Goes On At School.

And personally, I believe every word.

HIGH FINANCE

July 1st is New Year's Day—the first day of the new financial year.

It is a day for adding up assets and subtracting liabilities; a day for balancing last year's books and planning next year's budget. It is a day when farming families, wherever they may live, finally have to face the fiscal realities of their lives. It is also a day when those households, usually for the only time in the entire year, hold a Serious Talk About Money.

This talk can take many different forms because every couple has their own particular approach to financial discussions, ranging from benign inattention to a screaming match. But either way it is usually a totally futile exercise because of a widespread sociological phenomenon called the Law of Attracting Opposites.

This Law recognises that most domestic households contain one person who is good with money and one who is not, in the same way that punctual people always marry tardy people and night owls choose early birds. It is a cruel and mischievous trick of nature and nowhere does it cause more trouble than in the area of domestic finance.

I understand a new style of financial discussion has evolved lately, developed in desperation by the people who *Can* in an effort to deal with their partners who *Can't*. It is called the Treasurer syndrome and is quite effective. In our household it sounds something like this:

'What we need is Responsible Economic Management!'

'Yes, dear.'

'It's time to reign in the surge of weekly monetary aggregates!'

'Yes, dear.'

'Our tight credit situation necessitates strict budgetary controls!'

'But darling, don't we need a greater rate of capital inflow? An expansion of the (yawn) money supply?'

'No, we'll just have to reduce expenditure and raise our gross domestic product. And I wish you'd show a higher Rate of Interest!'

'Sorry, dear.'

New Year's Day is also a time for New Year's Resolutions, and here is mine: I swear by Dow Jones and all her little industrial averages that I will never again get myself into the financial mess I landed in not long ago.

It happened when my local country bank changed over to computers, which was all very fine and progressive—except they didn't tell me. So when my regular bank statement arrived I was in for a wonderful shock. My account was in the *black*. Hundreds of dollars OD. On Demand.

Now what would you do if you had more money than you thought you had? Yes, that's what I did. Trips to town, shops, restaurants, movies—then the next month's statment came. It was even more in the black!

After the third glorious month I began to have a few niggling doubts, so when the next statement arrived I studied it very carefully. OD. Perhaps it didn't stand for On Demand? But what else could it be? Off Duty? Outside Diameter? Over drive? *Overdraft*?

There was only one thing I could do to extricate myself from this hideous financial mess. I had to trick that computer as it had tricked me.

So I took my Bankcard and used it to get a cash advance for the amount of money owed, and paid off the debt. Then I paid Bankcard with my American Express card, I paid American Express with my Diners Club card, I paid Diners Club with my Barclaycard, and so forth and fifth. Finally I paid in my local library card—and that proved to be a master stroke. It fouled up the computer hook-up system for the entire area for three weeks—by which time I had managed to save up the amount of the original debt, and was in the clear.

But never again. From now on my account is going to stay in CR instead of OD although my expertise in financial management is BA.

But that financial fiasco did teach me something and

I'm going to pass it on to you, dear reader, in case you are the one in your household who is not financially gifted.

Forget about cash-flow budgeting. Forget about cost/price analysis. Avoid any Serious Talks About Money. Just remember this: if your outgo exceeds you income, your upkeep's your downfall. Happy New Year.

THAT'S ENTERTAINMENT

Everyone loves a party. Lunches, dinners, barbies, drinks—hospitality is a wonderful thing. The only trouble is that someday it must be repaid, and right now I am heavily in debt.

In fact, I'm so far behind in entertaining, that everyone I know, I owe. Whenever we go out nowadays (which is increasingly seldom—a sure sign of the above), I look around the room and realise with a cold, sinking feeling that everybody there has had us to their homes *since* they have been to ours.

Now in the never-actually-stated but nevertheless-universally-accepted rules of social intercourse, that means we Owe them. Society would disintegrate if people ignored this unwritten law of I-ask-you-so-you-ask-me-back. It is a timeless cycle, like the turning of the seasons.

Unfortunately, our friends are going through a drought. I can see I will have to gird my loins (of lamb) and give some dinner parties. But before I reach for the telephone to begin inviting people, there are some ethical questions about hospitality which I would like resolved.

For instance, what constitutes a Pay Back? Is an invitation in itself enough? If you have had some friends to dinner and then later on they ask you back and you can't go, do you consider they still Owe you? Or do you think they have discharged their obligation and that now you Owe them? In other words, does an Ask equal a Pay Back?

Life would be so much easier if it did. Whenever you heard of any friends planning to go away you could ask them out to dinner, safe in the knowledge that they would be unable to come. But they, having been Asked, would then Owe you again—and you would never be behind in your entertainment schedule.

Unfortunately, I don't think many people would buy that. I suspect most need to be actually wined, dined and reclined before they regard themselves as your debtor once more.

A Hen's Lunch is a good way of repaying hospitality—especially if some of the husbands don't get on, which is sometimes the case, strangely enough. But again, ethical questions arise. If you have eight women to lunch, have you in fact paid back eight couples? If so, it would be good value. You would be repaying 16 people while cooking for only eight. Two for the price of one.

But I don't think many couples would accept that either. For although his remark has been quoted out of context on countless occasions since, I'm sure Milton Friedman was actually discussing the above situation when he said there's no such thing as a free lunch.

Repaying hospitality is far easier for people who live in the city. Gourmet take-away food is readily available, and there is always a good little BYO restaurant around the corner where they can take their friends if they have neither the time nor the energy to cook.

But here in the country our nearest restaurant is many miles away, and could hardly be used as a dinner party venue. It is affectionately known in the district as The-Eat-It-And-Beat-It, or occasionally (and less poetically) The Chew-It-And-Spew-It.

The next nearest eatery is a Chinese cafe one town further on and known far and wide as The Golden Scours. I took a friend there one day recently. We were passing through the town about lunchtime, famished, so decided to risk a dim sim and a cup of coffee. As we ordered, the girl behind the counter asked: 'Do you wanna have it here or take it away?'

'Both, we hope,' answered my friend.

And speaking of friends, isn't that what it all boils down to—as a famous cook once said? With hospitality, good friends never keep count. True friends never tally the score. Real friends know that we all go through periods sometimes when we are too busy/

exhausted/broke to do much entertaining, and yet they keep having us back without waiting to be asked in return.

But one day, as another famous cook once said, the crunch will come. Those kind people who enjoy being your host must be repaid.

For there are two different meanings to the word 'host'. First, it means 'one who receives and entertains in his/her house or elsewhere'. Second, it means 'an animal upon which a parasite depends for existence'.

Perish the thought and pass me the phone.

A ROUND TUIT

As Mark Twain once said: 'Never put off till tomorrow what you can do the day after just as well.'

I am an incorrigible procrastinator. I delay, defer and postpone wherever I can, until now, after a lifetime's dedicated practice, I have raised the technique of putting things off to an art form.

Unfortunately, this skill causes endless trouble at home, because things either never get done at all or else they are left until the very bitter end, and are thus invariably accompanied by that great disturber of domestic tranquillity—the Last Minute Panic.

Every year I make a New Year's Resolution to do things immediately—but I always put off keeping it. The family says I should seek help from Procrastinators Anonymous—but I can't seem to get around to joining.

Truly, Hamlet was positively impetuous compared with me.

However, at long last I think my troubles may be over. My husband has given me the most amazing present for my birthday. It's called a tuit—a round one. I believe it will change my life.

You see, for years I've been saying: 'I'll do this or I'll do that—just as soon as I can get a round tuit.' So, now that I have a round tuit of my very own, I feel all sorts of jobs which have been crying out for attention, will at last be accomplished.

For instance, I will now be able to get to the bottom of the mending pile; throw out all the unmarried socks in the family's sock drawers; eliminate anything in the deep freeze with a Use By date expired for more than a year; write to the overseas rellies and thank them for the cards they sent last Christmas; name all the stray photographs lying around the house and stick them neatly into albums.

After that I will burn the naughty magazines in my

husband's shirt drawer before the children discover them; return the empty soft drink bottles cluttering up the laundry and collect their deposit; take the mountain of old newspapers out of the garage and tie it neatly into bundles ready to take to the Scout depot; actually take it to the Scout depot.

You see, all sorts of things are possible when you get a round tuit.

Out on the farm we can replace the cocky gate on the north boundary fence; install a water trough instead of the old bath in the stable yard; buy a new fuel cap to replace gladwrap-and-rubber-band on the ride-on mower; return the neighbour's super-spreader; (the list goes on and on, but I'm not allowed to finish it here as my husband says it's too embarrassing).

There are several other kinds of tuits available in life, such as the 'jump' and the 'in', not to mention the 'go' tuit. But personally, I think the round tuit is the most valuable of all, and I am determined to pass mine on, like a treasured heirloom, to my children.

For it seems to me, the big difference between life's Great Achievers and the rest of us, is that they *always*, however busy or whatever the task, get a round tuit.

Just think if Hamlet had had one? He'd be King of Denmark by now, living happily-ever-after with Ophelia at Elsinore, and Laertes a proud uncle.

I THINK THAT I SHALL NEVER SEE . . .

'To some people, a tree is something so incredibly beautiful that it brings tears to the eyes,' wrote William Blake. 'To others, it's just a green thing that stands in the way.'

Now that's all fine and dandy and causes no problems, except when these two kinds of people are married to each other—like us.

Our disagreement is not over paddock trees which we both love and cherish, but Trees Too Close To The House. This is because Trees Too Close To The House inevitably interfere with *drains*.

Drains are those parts of a homestead's lower digestive tract to which no-one pays the slightest attention until they *block up*. This invariably occurs when you're holding a party or a wedding, when you have elderly rellies in the house, or just before you leave for a fortnight's holiday.

Now being aware of this, I've always desisted from planting any new trees Too Close To The House, but I am spirited and vocal in my defence of existing arborial treasures.

The loveliest of these is an old willow, a tree so wonderfully green and shady in summer that just standing beneath it feels like taking a cool shower. Its proper name, of course, is a Weeping Willow. But my husband refers to it as a Weeping-Wailing-and-Gnashing-of-Teeth Willow.

This is because it grows in the back yard in an area of high density drainage and he believes it is solely responsible for the ever-increasing trouble we've been having lately with our drains.

After each blockage he threatens to chop it down, and only the most vociferous protestations, threats, cajolings, tears, hysterics and other forms of everyday wifely persuasion have managed to stay his hand thus far.

But last week came the end. With the bathroom basins again regurgitating superannuated toothpaste and the kitchen sink once more choking on last month's washing-up, the old willow finally faced extinction.

But when the moment came I, as any true tree lover would, threw myself around its trunk, begged for clemency and demanded proof of guilt. 'Okay,' declared its would-be executioner, reluctantly lowering his chain saw. 'If you want proof, it's in the drain.'

Now I've never been heavily into drains. They're men's work. (By the same token, my husband's never been heavily into mopping up after sick children in the middle of the night. That's women's work. This is not a sex-role thing, just an accepted division of responsibility.) So I was totally unprepared for what happened.

While he stood by imperiously giving me directions, I struggled to feed a long piece of hooked wire into the offending drain. When it struck the blockage I attached its end to an electric drill and gave it a burl.

Then, grabbing the wire firmly in both hands, I pulled on it as hard as I could. Nothing happened. I heaved and wrenched. It didn't budge. I hauled and strained and groaned and yanked and—suddenly the blockage gave way. The wire whipped out. And I landed flat on my back in the corner of the yard in a spray of black, primaeval ooze.

The first thing I saw as I clambered to my feet again, still dripping in oily, putrid, stygian slime, was my husband pouncing upon a wadded matt of willow roots which had emerged on the end of the wire. Scooping them up in both hands, he strode over and dangled them before me in triumph. 'I rest my case,' he said.

The execution did not take long. A short scream from the chain-saw, a crash of falling timber—and it was done. We loaded the body, green and broken, on to the back of the truck, and as it drove off towards the tip, I leaned against a fence post, and sang:
'I think that I shall never see,
A drain as lovely as a tree . . .'
My husband, turning to wave, laughed like a drain.

34

WHAT'S IN A NAME?

'In life there are many hundreds of common experiences, feelings, situations and even objects which we all know and recognise, but for which no words exist,' wrote Douglas Adams and John Lloyd.

'But on the other hand, the world is littered with thousands of spare words which spend their time doing nothing but loafing around on signposts pointing to places.'

Starting from this premise, these two English authors put together a little book called 'The Meaning of Liff' which I read recently with great delight. In it, they take a list of the names of English country towns and match them with things or situations in life for which no words exist. This means these place names 'can then start earning their keep in everyday conversation, and altogether make a more positive contribution to the English language.'

The result is great fun and a whole new vocabulary. I have compiled an Australian version for you:

Alice Springs: (verb) A hasty leap to safety over the cattle yards fence.

Borroloola: (noun) Small quantities of drench, vaccine, super or seed borrowed by neighbour and annoyingly never repaid.

Chatsworth: (n.) A lunch in town with The Gels.

Coldstream: (n.) The amount by which the depth of a puddle exceeds the height of your gumboot.

Coolaroo: (adj.) Descriptive of the pleasing coolness on the reverse side of the pillow.

Craigieburn: (v.) What the white sauce invariably does when the telephone rings.

Kadnook: (n.) The safe place you hide something then can't remember where it is.

Katamatite: (n.) A creek pebble which was shiny and interesting when wet and which is now a useless lump of rock which the children nevertheless insist on putting in the picnic hamper and dragging home.

Katherine Gorge: (n.) The massive three-course mid-morning blow-out enjoyed by a dieter who has already done her slimming duty by having a teaspoon of cottage cheese for breakfast.

Kaniva: (n.) A pestering child.

Innisfail: (adj.) Politely determined not to interfere. An innisfail expression can be seen on the face of a farmer watching a city visitor trying to work out how to open a lift-up gate.

Jambaroo: A jackaroo in a jam.

Lakes Entrance: The sheepyards in winter.

Lintrap: (n.) The question: 'What are you doing today?' If you reply, 'Nothing much,' the next question is sure to be: 'Then can you give me a hand in the shed/yards/paddock?'

Mildura: (n.) Something left over after a meal which you know you'll never use, but you shove in the 'fridge anyway and leave until it goes mouldy so you can then throw it out without feeling awful.

Natimuk: (n.) The liquid solution left at the bottom of the dip after dipping.

Mudgee: The sheepyards in spring.

Nullarbor: (n.) Someone who asks you a question then cuts off your answer by leaning forward and saying: 'I'll tell you why I asked . . .' and then talking solidly for the next half hour.

Port Fairy: (n.) An after-dinner drink for gays.

Rockhampton: (n.) The sheepyards in summer.

Rushworth: (v.) To clean up the house before the cleaning lady arrives.

Tumborumba: (n.) The ute starting up on a frosty morning.

Wantirna: (n.) The fourth wheel of a supermarket trolley which looks identical to the other three but renders the trolley completely uncontrollable.

Whyalla: (participial vb.) Standing in the kitchen wondering what on earth you went in there for.

Yackandandah: (n.) A person to whom, under dire injunctions of silence, you reveal your wheat yield when you want it much more widely known.

CONFESSIONS OF A COUNTRY STOVE

'Well, my dears, here I am all settled into my new country kitchen—home on the range, you might say. My surroundings, though lacking the polish and sophistication of many city kitchens, do possess a certain bucolic charm, and my family, though rather eccentric in many ways, are so thrilled and proud to have me that I am inclined to think kindly of them—so far.

My life here is hectic and exciting and nearly every moment of the day somebody in the family turns me on—if you'll pardon the expression. Occasionally when I've been working for hours Full On, cooking for the crutchers *et al.*, I dream of how easy life might have been if I'd gone to a city kitchen. But then I think how boring that would be. Do city stoves get to boil 5-in1 vaccine syringes on their hot plates? Do they hatch khaki campbell ducklings in their warming drawers? Do they revive hypothermal lambs in their ovens?

The Missus loves me dearly and though on occasion she is a little heavy-handed with the fryingpan and tends to grind rather than mix her sauces, she does try to keep my dials polished and my elements clean, and this I appreciate very much, because, as a famous stove once said, life wasn't meant to be greasy.

However, I don't see much of the man of the house. He did take some initial interest in me when I was being installed, fiddling with my dials, inspecting my warming drawers and even, you would believe, checking to see if there was a *bun* in my *oven*. But he hasn't been near me since.

Still, I'm not letting this upset me unduly, as I gather from my colleagues in other homestead kitchens that most farmers tend to ignore their stoves.

Strangely enough, he pays a great deal of attention

to the 'fridge, and what it contains—and I don't mean the marg. This, I understand, also is not uncommon amongst country men.

To be honest, I think the best part of being in this household is not what I do, but what I *hear*. My dears, it's *rivetting*! My rotisserie turns at what I overhear on occasions when The Gels come to lunch or when stock agents, company reps, or the local bank manager calls in for a cuppa and a chat.

As well, on most farms many of the major partnership investment decisions are made in the kitchen (a new hay baler versus a long-awaited holiday—you know the kind of thing) and these generate some fascinating family discussions. You learn a lot about human relationships in the kitchen.

Unlike Marie Antoinette, it was cake which brought me my good fortune. Apparently cake was a scarce commodity in this household before my arrival because, according to my Missus, my predecessor had a faulty oven and could not bake properly.

The Man harboured grave doubts about the oven being the real problem, but after years of suffering sponges like soggy pancakes and scones like little stones he decided Something Must Be Done!

So he asked a neighbour who was renowned for the excellence of her baking to come on over and test the oven. Now this placed the poor consultant cook in desperate zugswang, or a no-win situation.

If she achieved a magnificent cake out of the old oven, my Missus swore she would never speak to her again, and if she didn't, *he* wouldn't.

As it turned out, when the Big Bake-Off occurred, the cook's innate integrity forced her to make an honest attempt, but my Missus, suspecting fair play, took the precaution of substituting plain flour for the old S.R.— and yours truly was on order the very next day.

Given its history, then, you can imagine the tension which surrounded the occasion of *my* first cake—and, I flatly deny all responsibility for what happened. Was it my fault the Missus, though painstakingly careful in every other detail, forgot to grease the cake tin and the much-heralded *gâteau suprême* came out in tiny pieces?

Oh dear, I would have given my automatic timer to see the look on The Man's face that day when he opened up his lunch box out in the back paddock and beheld her *pieces de resistance*.

I am glad to report that since then the standard has improved somewhat but the poor dear was shell-shocked by the experience, and I notice from time to time that she still smuggles in homemade cakes bought from church stalls, rubs the price off to pretend they are hers, then pops them in the deep freeze to have on hand if needed—a kind of 'In Case of Emergency—Break the Gladwrap'.

The two smallest members of the family have been away for the past week, staying with friends. But that still leaves The Girl. Of all my rotten luck The Girl turns out to be interested in cooking and won't leave me alone. She and her cousin spent a whole day tormenting me, and ended up boiling a litre of milk over my two big tops. The Missus tried to be a good sport about it to the girls and said bad luck, it happens to everyone, etc., as she groped her way through the black smoke to the sink. However, when they'd departed, she let out a stream of language that frankly made me temporarily review my previous assessment of her as a real lady.

Lately I've not seen much of her. She and The Girl have been busy doing the feeding out on the farm, which though I understand is not arduous, is a large time commitment. Last night they only arrived home about 7 pm in the dark. 'I've just fed 4000 gaping mouths!' cries the Missus, throwing up her hands. 'And now here's five more awaiting their turn!' She then suggested a quick lap of the dining table with the oat-feeder may suffice, but the family did not agree, so yours truly was reluctantly called into service once more.

Still, despite the various culinary vicissitudes to which all cooks and therefore all stoves are prone, I find the life of a country stove is thoroughly delightful.

In fact, it's a piece of cake.

YOU'RE ONLY AS OLD AS YOU FEEL . . .

Society is obsessed with age. In every news bulletin you hear or newspaper story you read nowadays (particularly in the country press) age is highlighted as the primary factor in a person's life.

'Youth, 18, arrested for stealing farm petrol.'

'Woman, 38, finds rare bottle buried in creek.'

'Man, 42, injured in tractor accident.'

Do you think the exact age is relevant to these stories? Is it the *first* thing you should know about the people involved?

Why not say, 'Youth, angry and alienated, arrested for stealing farm petrol,' or 'Woman, astute and hardworking, finds rare bottle buried in creek' or even 'Man, careless and incompetent, injured in tractor accident'? Surely these kinds of factors have a greater bearing on the incidents than age?

If this trend of always quoting age continues, soon I expect to see such news items as: 'Youth, 18, arrested last week by an off-duty policeman, 48, was yesterday sentenced by a judge, 69, to six months' jail after the jury, 22, 38, 62, 27, 43, 56, 36, 44, 59, 32, 68, and 47 had found him guilty of stealing petrol from a farm bowser.'

The trouble is age doesn't necessarily tell you how old a person is. Ageing is a matter of attitude and performance, not chronology.

When Oliver Wendel Holmes, the great American writer, was 92, he used to take regular walks in the park with an old friend. One day a beautiful young girl passed by.

'Ah,' sighed Holmes in frank admiration. 'What I wouldn't do to be 70 again!'

We all know people who are old and world-weary at 17. And we all know others who are still young and vibrant at 65.

'I'm 65,' wrote James Thurber, 'and I guess that puts me in with the geriatrics. But if there were 15 months in each year, I'd be only 48. That's the trouble with us. We number everything.'

So what does it mean to be old? How can oldness be measured if not in years?

Certainly not by how many sheep you can still crutch per run or how many hours you can still sit at a tractor wheel—as many a young jackaroo with a hang-over will attest.

Eleanor Roosevelt said that, whatever your age, when you cease to make a contribution you begin to die. Henry Ford said you are old when you stop learning; Ogden Nash said you are old when you are sitting at home on a Saturday night and the telephone goes and you hope it isn't for you.

I think you are old when your get-up-and-go has got-up-and-gone.

I wonder if generations past were as prepossessed with age as we are? Can you imagine such headlines as: 'Captain Cook, 42, lands at Botany Bay!'? or 'John Batman, 34, says this is the place for a village!'?

It is interesting to note that of all the women mentioned in the Bible, the precise age of only one is mentioned. Sarah, wife of Abraham, is reported as giving birth to a son, Isaac, when she was 90 years of age.

Now that, I admit, is newsworthy.

But in most stories, the exact chronological tally of a person's life I believe is unnecessary. Surely broad descriptive terms such as 'young', 'middle-aged' or 'elderly' would do just as well?

I myself was born in the year of Our Lord only knows. I only ever admit to being plenty-nine.

A TASTE FOR LIFE

Let's face it, a gourmet is just a glutton with good manners. But by gorging delicately and by imbibing with grace and panache, a gourmet raises the bestial satiation of the appetite to an art form.

I hear a whisper that the latest *bon ton* in the country epicurian scene is the ability to distinguish a breed of cattle from the taste of its beef at table. Whether the beef is served as tournedos heloise, entrecote a la bordelaise, esterhazy rostbraten or plain old roast beef, the truly discerning country palate is now required to tell from its taste, colour and bouquet (just like a connoisseur of wine) which breed of beef is being served.

I wonder when this craze will hit the cities? All you gourmets and assorted bon-vivants in The Big Smoke will have to be prepared. You'll need a whole new range of graceful linguistics to be able to comment stylishly upon the origins of, say, the *petits filets de boeuf a la nicoise* in front of you. And remember, a good gourmet is ever 40% palate and 60% vocabulary.

In the country, it sounds like this: 'Hmmmm, this steak is pure hereford, autumn '85 drop, Cobungra strain I would say, grazed on the mountain country near Omeo. I detect this in the texture of the muscle which displays an attractive balance between the, uh, earthy sullenness of the valleys and the beguiling optimism of the mountain peaks. You will notice the colour is dark rather than deep and that this breed is characterised by a particularly pungent and free bouquet.'

'No, no, my friend. I think this steak is charolais, somewhat short on the nose, I'll admit, but giving better than it promises. The flavour is full of life, silky, yet serious and, er, how shall I say, introspective? Hmmm, I would say this charolais was dropped at Willaura, May '86, the Mount William Station breed to be exact.

It was grazed initially on the open plains south of the homestead, then fattened in the creek paddock beside the road. The phalaris pasture there gives that delightful piquancy to the aftertaste and is a characteristic of the region.'

'No, friends, never! This steak is neither charolais nor hereford. In my opinion it is simmental/santa gertrudis cross. And grain fed. Can't you taste the precocity of the feedlot hybrid? Just look at the marbling of fat through the muscle. This makes the texture stylish and especially supple with good deep colour and exemplary balance. It might perhaps incline towards coarseness near the bone, but never slumps into flabbiness. Hmmmm, the flavour is brisk, yet, how shall I put it, without a twang? All in all, an unashamedly raunchy little steak!'

So don't say you haven't been warned. The great beef debate is on the way.

However, to people like me who struggle to distinguish T-bone from topside, rump from round, the whole gourmet scene in the country has become far too esoteric. Why, some beef buffs are even claiming they can tell whether their filet mignon comes from a steer or a heifer.

But frankly, to me it's all bull.

THE NEW COMPUTER
(to be sung to the tune of 'Click Go The Shears')

Out in his office the young farmer sits,
Lost in a world full of Ks, bytes and bits,
Fixed is his gaze at the columns on the screen,
Struggling to puzzle out just what the hell they mean?

    Click goes the keyboard, click! click! click!
    Wild is his gaze and his hands move quick;
    His Missus looks around as she brings a cup of tea,
    And curses the inventor of the Apple II e.

Data base and DIF files, RAM and ROM and DOS,
Setting up a spread-sheet—getting hot and cross;
Escape to Desktop Menu, select, and press Return,
Computing looks so simple, but it's bloody hard to
    learn!

    Click goes the keyboard, click! click! click!
    His elbows are aching, his neck has a crick,
    His sheepdog looks around and is beaten by a blow,
    And curses the computer to obsess his master so!

The afternoon is over, the kid home from school
Runs to the computer, and draws up a stool,
'Having trouble, Dad?' he says. 'Can't you make it go?
Visicalc or Multiplan—what d'ya wanna know?'

    Click goes the keyboard, click! click! click!
    For kids it's so simple it fair makes you sick!
    Computing when you're older is medically a risk,
    Cursing at the curser may bring on a floppy disc!

EDUSPEAK—THE LANGUAGE OF TEACHERS

If your child is about to start school for the first time, you will need to learn a whole new language: Eduspeak, the language of teachers.

Eduspeak has evolved in both urban and rural areas over the past decade to help understanding and communication between teachers, and to mystify and terrify parents. Although originally an off-shoot of English, its word patterns and grammatical structures bear only a faint resemblance to the mother tongue today.

But parents need to speak this language in order to find out what is being taught in the classroom so that they can help their children with their homework. Or, as it would be said in Eduspeak: 'parents require an ongoing overview of the practical and conceptual skills derived from the classroom situation in order to provide meaningful and supportive reinforcement of the facilitators and inhibitors of the cognitive process in the home situation.'

I have made a detailed study of Eduspeak and discovered it has certain basic rules which are simple to apply. These I am willing to share with you, so that when you attend your first parent/teacher interview you will not go through the humiliation I suffered by speaking only English. Learn these rules carefully and you will be able to converse in fluent Eduspeak with any teacher at your school, and even, given practice, the principal.

First, never use a simple word where a complicated and obscure one will do. Second, use the key words of Eduspeak in your sentences at every opportunity. The most important of these key words are 'skill' and 'situation'.

Now apply these rules concurrently and English becomes Eduspeak at once. For example, 'Julia reads at home' becomes 'Julia is developing her oracy skills in the ambience of the home situation'; or 'Eda is learning swimming' becomes 'Eda is acquiring flotation and propulsion skills in a water environment situation'. You see?

Other important key words to be used wherever possible are 'ongoing interaction' and 'meaningful overview'; or 'meaningful interaction' and 'ongoing overview'; or 'overacted interview' and 'meaningful goings-on'.

However, let me warn you to exercise some restraint with the 'situation' situation lest you find yourself in an embarassing lexical repeat situation or even in an undignified comedy situation, or, as it is better known, situation comedy.

Next you must memorise some common Eduspeak phrases to sprinkle throughout your sentences: 'self-actuating motivation', 'appropriate verbal mediators' and 'uncrystallised cognitive reward structures' to name just a few. These pearly gems will fit into almost any context and can be added to the key words if extra levels of sagacity are called for: thus, 'self-actuating motivation skills' and 'appropriate verbal mediator situations', etc.

It may take some practice, but in good Eduspeak you must eliminate prepositions from your conversation. Two nouns locked together are the hallmark of fluency in this language. Never refer to the effectiveness of teachers, but to teacher-effectiveness; never the participation of parents, but to parent-participation; remember to say student-satisfaction, peer-group pressure, role-perception and process-evaluation.

Finally, learn to make nouns into verbs wherever possible. You must prioritise, categorise, access and action, and refer not to being a parent, but to parenting. You will hear much about concerned parenting and even, on occasion, concerned grand-parenting. I believe this should be extended to include concerned aunting and uncling, and certainly concerned sistering and brothering (or should it be sibling-ing?).

Now you have the basic rules of Eduspeak, the language of teachers, let me point out that I only promised to explain how to speak it, not how to understand it. For that, dear reader, I'm afraid you're on your own and I cannot help. Frankly, what it all actually *means*, I have not the slightest idea.

LIVING IN A DROUGHT

Has anyone seen our farm? It disappeared two weeks ago in a gale of wind and was last seen heading towards Melbourne a hundred metres in the air.

Perhaps it landed in Collins Street and gave a whole new meaning to the term 'Collins Street Farmer'?

Perhaps it spread out over your area and you have been dusting it off your furniture and vacuuming it out of your carpets ever since? If so, would you please empty your dustbin into a postpack and mail it back to us?

If a duststorm in the city makes you wonder about conditions in the country, let me tell you what it's like living in a drought. A crop without water is described in farmers' jargon as having 'moisture stress'. At the moment the crops are not alone in suffering this condition. Farming families have it too.

'Moisture stress' makes the husk dry and shrivelled, the heads quite empty and the stalks bend and droop in the sun. Exactly.

Our basic problem of course, is lack of Wholly-And-Totally-Essential-Resource—or W.A.T.E.R., as city people call it. Living in a drought means showering every third day for ten seconds with the plug in, bathing the children in the same water then siphoning it down to the kitchen to use for cooking the vegetables. When the vegetables are done, you drain the water into the sink, wash up in it, rinse out the tea-towels, then ladle it back into a saucepan and serve it up as soup next day.

Sometimes this soup turns out thin like consomme and sometimes it is thick like mulligatawny or even, on occasion, vichyssoise. But it is usually quite palatable given imaginative use of herbs and condiments—but no salt.

Living in a drought means using bore water (the

fresh-water dam and tanks are dry) and bore water usually has such a high natural salt content that the sea tastes like moselle by comparison.

When you wash your hair in this bore water and comb it into place, it stays that way for a week in even the strongest winds. When you stir your coffee the spoon remains upright in the cup, and after being rinsed in it, all your vegemite glasses come out Lalique.

Living in a drought means the constant pursuit of dust. After sweeping the floors each day you need not a dust pan and brush, but a wheel-barrow and shovel to scoop it all up. It means taking the clothes down off the line and re-washing them every time a vehicle or a mob of sheep goes past the back gate, yet over the weeks watching every garment you own grow slowly and inexorably *fawn*.

Living in a drought means being obsessed by the weather. When the barometer drops and dark clouds gather you go through an agony of suspense wondering if at last this time it will RAIN! You prowl constantly around the homestead watching the sky, tasting the wind, and children and small dogs know to keep well away.

Now I know that city people are not unaffected by a drought. I know you too have suffered from severe water restrictions. So next time you're watering your garden with a hand-held hose between 7 and 9 pm, please spare a thought for the people in the country who are down to hand-held face-washers between 7 and 7.05 pm.

Then, instead of posting our farm back to us, why not deliver it personally? Travel out here and experience for yourself what it is like living in a drought?

Come to lunch. We will give you some soup.

NEVER BET ON A CERTAINTY

Have you ever noticed that whenever people say they are absolutely certain, sure and *positive* about something—actually they are not?

If a person states a simple fact, you can accept it. But if that person tells you he is dead sure and utterly positive about that fact, beware! From my observations, extreme protestations of certainty invariably mean a person is racked by inner doubt.

I call this syndrome Verbal Overkill (*VOK*) and if you train yourself to recognise it you will have an advantage in many potentially perilous situations.

Here is an example: you are rushing off to town and you need some more petrol for the car and the key to the farm bowser is missing. If your partner says: 'I'm sure I left it on the hook inside the garage door! I'm *positive* I did!' you should recognise at once that he can't remember where on earth he left that key and is suffering acute inner turmoil. The next step is calmly to suggest perhaps he look in the glove box of the ute or the pocket of his molies or his Driza-Bone. A measure of true maturity is resisting making any comment when he inevitably finds the key therein.

The VOK syndrome operates in all areas of life from the farmer who tells his bank manager he is absolutely positive there will be an early break and his wheat crop will go three tonnes this year, to the stud breeder who assures his clients he is utterly certain that the sire for which he's just paid a fortune will throw top progeny.

VOK is the oral manifestation of wishful thinking. It is a kind of verbal hoping against hope. Butchers (I'm quite certain this steak will be tender, lady), vets (don't worry—she's sure to be on her feet again in a day or two') and machinery repairmen (I'm absolutely positive

it'll give you no more trouble now') all use VOK constantly. Race-horse trainers and used-car salesmen
could not operate without it, and clergymen when discussing the Hereafter have refined it to an art form.

Politics wallows in VOK and it is possible to assess
with great accuracy just how confident a politician really is about his chances in a forthcoming election from
his VOK-quotient. If he says: 'Yes, I will win,' you
know he really believes this to be the case. If he says:
'I'm sure I will win,' you know he thinks he has some
chance. But if he says: 'There's no possible doubt! I'm
an absolute certainty!' it means he is actually worried
stiff.

Big business is not immune from VOK. If the chairman of a company in which you have invested your life
savings tells the share-holders at the annual general
meeting that next year his company will pay a dividend, take heart. But if that chairman says 'next year I
am quite certain we will pay a dividend' sell, sell, sell!

VOK is just as prevalent in the country, too. If we
have a visitor to our farm who simply says, 'yes, I can
ride', we give him a bridle and point him at the horse
paddock. But if he says he is an extremely accomplished rider with absolutely years of practise in the
saddle, the only horse he's offered is Shank's pony.

If I my husband asks me can I give him a hand up at
the woolshed to draft a mob of ewes, and he says: 'It'll
take about twenty minutes—they're running well,' I
pop my cake in the oven and head off without a care.
But if he says: 'I'm absolutely positive it'll only take a
jiffy—this mob is never, ever any trouble!' I prepare to
spend the entire morning running in circles in the dusty
yards.

It is especially advisable to be aware of VOK when
discussing any major investment decisions on the farm.
If your partner says: 'We need a new tractor', then you
might as well start perusing the brochures without ar-
gument. But if he says: 'We simply *must* have a new
tractor! The old one is completely and utterly obsolete!'
you can bet all he really wants is a tractor which has a
new stereo-system and an air-conditioned cab.

There are some universal and historical country classics

of which everyone should beware: 'You couldn't possibly get bogged in that paddock!' and 'I'm absolutely *certain* you have enough petrol to get home!' or 'You haven't a worry in the world! That bull is docile as a baby!'

Wherever you travel on life's Great Highway you are sure to come across some poor stranded motorist whose partner was absolutely *positive* the frayed fanbelt would last another 1000 k's.

So learn to watch out for VOK and your life will be far easier.

That you will need my advice on this matter is something of which I am sure, positive and have not the slightest doubt in the world!

HOW YOU GONNA KEEP 'EM . . .

When the cows have trouble calving, the sheep are fly-blown, and it hasn't rained in memory, country people sometimes yearn to Get Away, breathe in a lungful of pollution, wake in the mornings and hear the birds cough, and generally immerse themselves in the flesh-pots of a big city.

We did this last weekend.

The trip had been planned for a long time for a treat for the children while their father was away overseas, and I promised to expose them to as many city sights, sounds and sensations as possible. They were taut with excitement.

Our home is nearly 400 k's from Melbourne, and long car trips are always an ordeal with young children. We set off after school on Friday, and only 30 k's down the highway came the inevitable question: 'How much further?' So we played five games of I-Spy, seven games of Guess-the-number-plate, three games of Count-the-windmills and one of white horses, which was a failure as there weren't any.

By Skipton I was suffering acute noise fatigue so I told the children there would be a Mars bar for anyone who could sit for five minutes with their right hand high in the air and their left hand holding their lips together. It worried me for the success of their future lives that they swallowed this ploy—but the five minutes' silence was bliss.

Our hotel was situated right in the heart of the city, and when at last we arrived we were all exhausted and ready for bed. But getting the children off to sleep was another matter (our rooms were adjoining—the two girls in one, and James and myself in the other); the roar of the traffic, the bustle of people, the flashing neon lights. Just as I'd managed to get them all settled down and mildly drowsy a police car or an ambulance would scream past, and it was up and out of bed and over to the window for a look.

'There's a gang of robbers!' cried Eda, pointing to a group of rather pleasant-looking teenage boys below. 'I bet that man's about to murder someone!' said James, pointing to a well-dressed businessman crossing the street. Oh television, I thought, you have so much to answer for!

Next morning we set out to explore the sights of the city. 'Look at the taxis! Look at the traffic lights!' Children from the country who treat tiger snakes, creeks in flood or wild cattle with disdain, have no idea how to cope with crowds or heavy traffic, and so merely crossing the road was a hair-raising experience. So I told them that the rules of the bush also apply to the concrete jungle—if you get lost *stay put*, and dressed the three of them alike so I could ascertain their continued presence at a glace.

Into the teeming arcades and department stores we went, where to my surprise the escalators proved of far greater interest than the merchandise; the Mall, the City Squre, the Town Hall and Cathedral, plus tram rides without number.

The only multi-storey building near our home is 60 k's away and boasts only two floors, so a visit to the Regent Hotel in Collins Street was mandatory. Up, up, up we went in the lift (lifts are another endless thrill) to the 35th floor where we had been advised the ladies' washroom provided the best view in Melbourne.

Of course James presented a problem in this regard, but we tied a scarf around his head, draped him in beads and gave him my handbag to carry, and happily he accompanied us into the ladies' in drag.

The view from there was one of (dare I say it?) Unparalleled Grandeur. The mildness of the day and the air's blue haze softened the square edges of the city skyline and we were all enchanted.

'Look at the people like little ants!' said Julia. 'Look at the matchbox cars!' said Eda. 'What an ace train set!' said James, pointing towards Flinders Street railway yards. 'Do those trains really work?' 'Well, sometimes they do, sometimes they don't . . . ' I murmured, and turned away.

We lunched with friends in Fitzroy and the children experienced the common city frustration of trying to play cricket in a tiny backyard. Then, resolved that they should have at least one dose of culture, we headed off to the National Gallery in St. Kilda Road. There a kind and extremely brave voluntary guide offered to show us around, but children are ever their own guides, and they rushed around hither and yon as different works of art caught their eye.

They were awe-stuck with the delicacy of the glass collection, loved the early Australian landscapes and thought the modern abstract expressionists hilarious. They lay flat on their backs on the floor of the Great Hall and gazed up in awe at its magic ceiling, and after studying the sculpture courtyard announced that Rodin's 'Balzac' looked like their music teacher at school, and Henry Moore's 'Big Lizzie' looked like— me.

From the gallery we drove on to the Fun Factory—the sublime to the gorblimey, you might say. This was a children's entertainment centre in South Yarra—a multi-coloured musical hell-hole of pin-ball machines, computer games, side-shows and a roller-skating rink.

'No drinking! No swearing! No visible tattoos allowed!' said a big sign outside, which immediately made us wonder who had *invisible* tattoos—and *where*!

The children spent a fortune smash, bash, crashing the dodgem cars, buuurrrmmmmmmming the radio-controlled racers and shooting life-sized, unarmed Indians in the shooting gallery. Garish, phrenetic, with a noise level well above the threshold of pain, to me it was all a mindless, psychedelic Sodom and Gommorah. But yes, you guessed. The children just loved it.

That evening, because I presumed the adventures of the day to have sapped their excess exuberance, I decided to take the children to a proper restaurant for dinner. Changing beforehand back at the hotel I lectured them about the importance of good manners in a first-class restaurant—or, indeed, anywhere.

In terms of behaviour modification, I believe in both the carrot and the stick. So I announced that tonight two rules would apply: for careless eating I would administer A-Slap-A-Slop (the stick) and for refinement and grace I would present a Neatest-Eater-Award, (the carrot).

As it turned out, I needn't have worried. The dim lights and sophistication of the restuarant had the effect of bringing out in the children an exaggerated and wondrous gentility. As they sipped their lemonade from stemmed glasses the girls crooked their little fingers in a nauseous curve, and James stuck his out at right-angles—like a lightning conductor.

Then came the menu. I blanched when Eda ordered fish 'n' chips and James asked for bangers 'n' mash, but the waiter (a true professional) blinked not an eye-lid, just calmly directed them to a suitable choice.

Next morning over breakfast we discussed our plans for the day. The Zoo? The Old Melbourne Gaol? Ripponlea? Puffing Billy? Longingly I suggested the Botanic Gardens or Wattle Park? 'But we live in a park!', cried the children, and thinking of our rolling redgum paddocks back home I had to agree.

So we opted for the Victoria Market instead. The children were enthralled at the press of people, the bustle and business, and all the different languages bubbling in the air. Foolishly I had promised they could buy something there to take home, and so we raced through the throng from stall to stall.

Julia chose a fluffy buff-coloured rabbit-skin overcoat with little feet for buttons. Eda wanted a black satin jumpsuit with gold sequins all around the neck, and black patent-leather high heels to match. James fell for a luminous painting of a negro girl with braided hair and gorgeous bare bosoms. What we actually brought home were three white mice.

By lunchtime we were famished and the question arose of where to eat, but there was only one place the children wanted to go—McDonald's. Country children believe they are deprived by having so little junk food. Everything they eat is so boringly healthy; home-grown vegetables, fresh-killed meat, and fruit bottled from the farm orchard. So I weakened, and off we went to McDonald's in Victoria Parade.

Chicken-and-chips, fish burgers, Big Macs, thick-shakes—they devoured them all with gusto. The place was crowded and a strange man had to squeeze in to our table to eat his lunch. 'Oh, look!' said James in a loud voice. 'That man has a big wart on his nose!' 'Hush,' I hissed. 'He can hear you.' 'But doesn't he *know* he has a big wart on his nose?' replied James. It was time to leave.

By mid-afternoon the children had had enough. They were tired and satiated by so many new sights, sounds and sensations. They wanted to go home. 'What did you all like best?', I asked in the car as we headed off, interested to hear their impressions. 'I liked the Art Gallery,' said Julia, which surprised me. 'I liked the Fun Factory,' said James, which didn't. 'I liked being waited on at the restaurant,' said Eda, and I agreed whole-heartedly.

But as we drove on and on and darkness fell, the spaces widened and the stars came out (do city people ever see the stars?) we all decided that the very *best* part of a visit to the city was returning home to the country once again.

CLEARING SALES

'Sale-O!, Sale-O!,' calls the auctioneer, and up jumps the pulse rate of every serious bargain-hunter and dedicated junk-collector like me at a country clearing sale.

I love clearing sales. I love the crowds, the atmosphere, the excitement. Comparing a country clearing sale to its city counterpart—the garage sale—is like comparing an eastern bazaar to a corner store. And for an afternoon's entertainment, it has no equal.

However, like all human commercial endeavour it has its own ground rules, its own trading traditions, and it is wise to know the form before you go. Afterall, unless you're on a horse you don't want to be taken for a ride.

When you arrive at a clearing sale everything is laid out before you in rows in the home paddock. The first section is the big equipment known as Machinery and Plant: tractors and trucks, headers and slashers, augers and ploughs. It is a wonderfully colourful assembly of metal muscle, all steam cleaned and polished to within an inch of its life.

The next section is Furniture and Household Effects and often comprises an amazingly diverse range of items. This is because nothing is ever thrown away in the country and the offering may be the accumulation of generations, cleaned out from cellars, attics, garages, barns and sheds all around the property.

In this section a likely offering might be: bassinet and stand (chrome); lounge suite (vinyl): lady's writing desk (walnut); B & W TV; 2 electric jugs; 6 bentwood chairs; magazine rack; gentleman's wardrobe (cedar); butter churn; high chair (chrome); stroller (chrome); andirons (brass); and always, always, a collection of dusty Fowler's bottling jars.

My favourite section of a clearning sale is the last,

and is known as Sundry Items Too Numerous To Mention. This section actually is of least importance to the vendor—but to a junk collector it is paradise: old books, records, paintings, ornaments, lamps, cutlery and crockery, clocks, photographs (old), bottles (old), toys (old) and sometimes even pets (old).

When you browse amongst any of these sections, you should do so with a nonchalant air. Never reveal interest in an item. If you spot a Ramued drip glaze jug amongst the pile of chipped Noritaki, leave it there untouched. Do not draw attention to the leather-bound first edition by separating it from the Mills and Boon, and until bidding commences leave the sterling fiddle-pattern teaspoons nestling amongst the collection of faded EPNS.

Also, don't spend all your time in one section. If you are interested in the deep freeze or the kero heater (new wicks), spend most of your time inspecting the off-set discs (with remotes) or the super-spreader (six-bag capacity) remembering, of course, to kick the occasional tyre in passing.

This kicking should be done nonchalantly but with some care. Many's the toe been bruised or even broken because it struck rim instead of rubber on a wheel.

Next are the assessment procedures. To assess the value of an item accurately requires some careful detective work. For the history of a tractor, for example, ignore any readings on the hours meter. You will gain a far better indication of its actual working life by checking the wear on the clutch pedal, the amount of paint rubbed off from around the fuel cap and how much padding is left in the seat.

Bidding techniques are most important. Bidding is a verbal game of nerves between you and the opposition, with the auctioneer as referee. It is a mental tennis match, and it requires great skill and concentration to volley bids back and forth through the air while the heads of the watching crowd turn from side to side—like spectators at the Davis Cup.

There are two schools of thought on successful bidding. Some people shout their bids like a battle cry, hoping to frighten the opposition into early withdrawal and defeat. Others prefer the quiet, anonymous approach, and register their bids by nothing more than a flicker of the third lash of their left eye. Because of the predominance of the latter technique it is most important when you are *not* bidding to keep perfectly still. Careless gestures such as brushing a fly from your face or rubbing your ear may render you the proud owner of an 800-bag wheat silo, 14 k's of high-tensile fencing wire or a $100,000 open-front header.

There is a widely-held fallacy that because you buy something at a clearing sale, *ergo,* it must be cheap. Many's the unwary buyer who has proudly taken home some old 'bargain' only to discover later on that he has paid over new price for it. So have some idea of values before you go. Even in the country, no-one likes to find themselves up the creek.

For me, a clearing sale is an exciting and rewarding commercial experience and is worth travelling many a country mile to attend. It has other things to offer besides, but I won't list them all here. They are Sundry Items Too Numerous to Mention.

THE DREADED
WHENEYE . . .

Are you ever bothered by wheneyes? I run into them wherever I go and I find them boring and annoying.

Wheneyes occur both in the country and in the city, and in every walk of life; at work, at parties, in education, in government, in sport—even in the media. And one of the most exasperating things about them is that it's impossible to pick them from outward appearances. This makes them difficult to avoid.

A wheneye is a person whose conversation is dominated by the phrase: 'When I . . . '

'When I was in Katmandu last spring . . .'

'When I won Grand Champion at the Sydney Royal . . .'

'When I had lunch with Alan Bond. Sorry, when I *last* had lunch with Alan Bond . . .'

Wheneyes are more annoying than blowflies at a barbeque—and just as persistant. There should be some kind of repellant spray to use against them. A blatant yawn, which would mortify a more sensitive soul into immediate silence, seems to bother them not at all.

Another maddening characteristic of wheneyes is that they always pre-suppose (usually correctly) that where they have been and what they have done, you have not. They can somehow tell you haven't been Away for ages, and what with a run of poor seasons and a new tractor you have no immediate prospect of doing so.

So when a wheneye says 'When I was in Capri last summer . . . ' it is especially irritating because you *know* he knows you haven't been further than Port Fairy. And he knows you know he knows.

The irony of it is that interesting people are clever enough never to mention their exotic travels, career successes, important connections or prowess at work/ sport/sex without first being *asked*. Then, when forced to tell what they're actually dying to tell anyway, they can give the same description as the most boring wheneyes—and their audience will be rapt and enchanted.

Wheneyes come in all shapes and sizes. A school-age wheneye can be pretty hard to take: 'When I got straight A's in maths . . . '

Elderly wheneyes also can be irritating. For instance, you race back to the laundry from the sheep yards to pile another load of dirty clothes into the washing machine, and your ageing relative murmurs. 'When I was your age I had to boil up the copper and make my own soap . . . '

To those who are overweight, a weight-watching wheneye can anger to the point of violence. 'Last winter when I was 82 kilograms . . . ', she says as she's standing in front of you thin as a stick. And you suspect she's only said it because she knows you've been living on carrot juice and lettuce leaves for six weeks and haven't lost a gram.

I suppose society has been plagued by wheneyes since time began. Certainly there is evidence around to suggest it, like the great hymn: 'When I survey the wondrous cross . . . ' or Milton's great poem: 'When I consider how my light is spent . . . '

But I suppose nothing much can be done about them. The rest of us will just have to go on suffering in silence while they bore us to tired sobs. Which reminds me of the time last year when I . . . ooh, sorry.

*   *   *

TAXES

The people in Australia who think that taxes are too high are divided into two groups: men and women. Everyone agrees the tax burden is excessive. As far as I can see, the only difference in this country today between a tax collector and a taxidermist is that the taxidermist leaves the skin.

If the great American statesman Patrick Henry thought taxation without representation was bad, he should see how bad it is *with* representation. It is becoming increasingly difficult for us all to support Canberra in the manner to which it has become accustomed. The government seems to regard each of us as someone who has what it takes.

Now, given that some degree of taxation is essential and should be cheerfully and honestly paid, I would like to venture some suggestions for changes to our taxation laws, changes which, if implemented, would result in a more equitable and beneficial system of raising revenue, one which would have a positive rather than a negative effect on the community.

The main problem with our present system, it seems to me, is that excessive rates on personal income mean that taxes have become, in effect, a fine for doing well. So why not change direction and impose those fines not on initiative and hard work as at present, but on bothersome areas of life?

For instance, I would like to see a tax on all broken promises. On past performance, a tax on politicians' broken promises alone would go a long way towards eliminating the national debt. And if, every time a plumber, electrical repairman or kitchen renovator made a commitment and failed to keep it, he were required to pay tax on it, think what a bonanza that would be for the Treasury?

Next I propose a Meetings Tax. The age of consensus

has generated a plethora of meetings, and I suggest a tax should be placed on each to ensure it has not been called unless really necessary—which is certainly not the case in my experience. Also, through its sub-sections, this tax could help meetings become more efficient and effective, by imposing special levies on the banes of all meetings: those people who only attend when they wish to complain; those who stay silent throughout a meeting — then go outside and complain; those who cheerfully vote in favour of everything but volunteer to help with nothing; and especially those who pledge their whole-hearted suppport for your proposal before a meeting, then, at the meeting when your motion is put, sit on their hands.

Under present tax laws the Government gathers revenue by imposing heavy excise duties on beer and spirits—then raising all other taxes to drive you to drink. But I think it would have a far more salutary effect on the community if a tax were placed on anti-social behavior instead.

For instance, why not tax people who are continually late, who jump their place in a queue, or who never answer invitations? Why not tax people who talk for hours on public telephones when there is a crowd waiting outside, who never turn up to help at club working bees, or who ask you for a lift in your car when they have a heavy head cold?

On the domestic scene, instead of an assets tax, I suggest an Annoying Habits Tax which would not only be a great revenue-raiser but also have a wonderfully soothing effect upon family relationships.

This tax could be collected from people who, for instance, wear their muddy gumboots inside the house, remove the biro from beside the telephone, leave the tops off textas and the toothpaste, rumple the morning newspaper before you have a chance to read it, constantly avoid the washing-up or, sin of sins, use the last of the lavatory roll and fail to replace it.

In the country, I would like to see a gate tax imposed on every farm gate which fails to unfasten without barking your knuckles or swing open without scraping your shins. As well, a special penalty should be imposed for swearing at dogs and wives in the sheep yards, and a severe fine exacted for all homestead equipment (buckets, towels, carving knives, garden hoses, etc.) stolen for use in the woolshed and not returned.

I would also like to see a special retrogressive tax for transport drivers who do not turn up when they say they will, and agricultural department extension officers or chemical company salespersons who turn up without saying they will.

Of course the essential factor in any reform must be to stop penalising success. And if the above suggestions were implemented immediately, there would be no need for the recently-imposed Capital Gains Tax. Besides, didn't we have one before? I mean, when we sent our taxes to Canberra—didn't the capital gain?

But the last part of my tax package is the most important of all. I suggest that, as with all other consumer legislation, the taxation department be required to offer us our money back if we are not satisied.

EVERYTHING'S RELATIVE

When Edward Gibbon wrote 'our relations to each other are various and infinite,' he might have been commenting on life in this country today. In Australian society, whether urban or rural, it seems that everyone and everything are related.

At least that's the impression you gain from listening to politicians. They all use the word 'relation' or the phrase 'in relation to' more than any others in their entire political vocabulary (with the possible exception of 'I promise'). To hear them speak, Australia is just one big happy family.

For instance, they talk about our public relations, private relations, business relations and Government relations—not to mention commercial relations, trade relations, sporting relations and foreign relations.

Then there's primary industry in relation to secondary industry, exports in relation to imports, tariffs in relation to bounties, production in relation to demand, research in relation to extension, and orderly marketing in relation to free trade.

On our farms we have equity in relation to debt, pasture in relation to cropping, fuel consumption in relation to horse-power and micron in relation to yield.

On our roads we have fleets of trucks in relation to rail, and on our wharfs we have groups of piers in relation to ships—or, as they are better known— piergroup relationships.

This remarkable network of kith and kin spreads out to permeate every sector of daily life and endeavour. We have city/country relations, broker/client relations, doctor/patient relations, parent/teacher relations, and employer/employee relations.

This latter group is referred to as our Industrial Relations and they are a particularly important but rather touchy branch of the national family, made up of two diverse filial factions known as Harmonious and Chaotic.

In our private lives we have distant relations, blood relations, business relations and personal relations. This latter group is divided into sexual and non-sexual relations (the 'non' being French for 'no' and is what you must keep saying to maintain this type of relations).

Even our national financial affairs are part of a glorious lineage of relations. Profits are in relation to taxes, taxes are in relation to the budget, the budget is in relation to the deficit, and the deficit is in relation to the economy.

Perhaps politicians talk like this because they think it makes people feel all warm and cosy inside having so many relations?

But personally I believe that out here in the country we'd all be far better off if we had fewer relations—and more friends.

A CHRISTMAS WISH

Dear Santa Claus,

The children are busy writing to you with their annual Christmas hopes and dreams so I thought I would slip in a note too, because there seems to be some misunderstanding between us.

This time last year, if you remember, I wrote asking *please* no more sexist gifts for Christmas. I didn't mean to whinge but at the time I had on hand a great accumulation of tea towels, frilly aprons, casserole dishes, lace doiles, flowery gardening gloves and colour co-ordinated face washer/shower cap sets. Now I suppose you could argue a casserole dish or a tea towel is not necessarily sexist because (some) men use them. But Santa, how many men have to suffer them as *gifts*?

So last Christmas morn, supremely confident that my letter would gain you complete sympathy and co-operation, I arose at first light with the children and crept down to the playroom where we have our Christmas tree. What a magnificent array of presents you had brought in the night! All shapes, sizes and colours, and all wonderfully tantalising in their bright wrappings.

While the family dressed and gathered for The Opening Ceremony, I teased myself with the possibilities of that colourful array. What might there be for me? Tureck's recording of Bach's Forty-Eight? The latest Elizabeth Jolley? A new tennis racquet? Or even a dozen Rosemount Chardonnay?

Afterall, those are the kinds of gifts my husband receives—and for any of them I would give my eye teeth.

Imagine, then, how I felt as I unwrapped my parcels on Christmas morning and discovered: an angle-grinder and an orbital sander!

Really and truly, Santa. Yes, I know they are wonderfully efficient and certainly not sexist.

But I am not heavily into angle-grinding OR orbital

sanding (as I suspect you know). I grant you those Phillip's-head screwdrivers with the yellow insulated handles will be useful and there are several jobs around the house I can complete now I have that lovely multi-purpose soldering gun. But seriously, Santa, for what do I require a 39-piece socket set with combination ¼″ and ⅜″ drive features, a/F, whitworth and metric⸮

I have a sneaking suspicion that you and your little elfin friends up at the North pole enjoyed a great deal of merriment and glee at my expense. I can imagine you all sitting around sipping Christmas spirit and rocking with laughter—Ho! Ho! Ho!—each time you decided on another of my presents.

The final straw came when, with the family's mirth at my expense bordering on the hysterical, I grabbed the last parcel in my pile and immediately felt through the bright red wrapping—a book! Oh joy! At last a decent present! What might it be⸮ The Macquarie Thesaurus⸮ Hughes' 'Fatal Shore'⸮ It didn't much matter. To me, all books are wonderful.

In a fever of excitement I ripped off the paper and discovered: the Complete Workshop Manual for an International Nine Series five-ton tip truck.

So this Christmas, Santa, could we call it quits⸮ I have learnt my lesson. Any one of those dreary domestic gifts you used to bring me would be preferable to last year's lot. Besides, our household has run very short of hand towels, our large wooden salad bowl has been broken and we desperately need a new coffee pot.

Happy Christmas,

Fussy Boots,
Balmoral.

SIGNS OF THE TIMES

A professor of English recently introduced to his class what he termed one of the finest, most elegant lines of poetry in the English language. 'Walk with light,' he quoted. 'Walk with light. Now isn't that a beautiful line?' The class agreed and wanted to know the author.

'I don't know,' he replied. 'I read it on a sign at a pedestrian crossing.'

According to a recent survey by the Australian Road Research Board most people in the community (unlike the good professor) do not notice road signs. They simply do not see them.

I suppose the reason for this is that there are so many signs on our roads nowadays, after a while they lose their power to catch the eye and command attention. This is horrifically dangerous, if you think about it.

So lately, in the interests of safety, I have made a special effort to notice the road signs I come across both on city and country roads. I have been well-rewarded. For instead of a mere set of safety instructions, I have discovered in road signs a whole new form of modern literary expression—the one-line cautionary tale. Taken literally, I find they offer not only road rules but also much wise counsel for life.

For instance, many an over-worked farmer could avoid an impending coronary if only he were to heed the double warning implicit in a SLOW DOWN sign— or even a STOP! Kids tempted to try drugs should be warned that it's a ONE WAY STREET, and if they go ahead then it's a STEEP DESCENT.

Political parties seeking to hold the middle ground should take note of NO LEFT TURN or NO RIGHT TURN, and party leaders discourage any leadership challenges with NO STANDING ANYTIME! (Certainly John Howard should remember that some of his backbenchers are SLIPPERY WHEN WET.)

In the area of marriage, what better advice could there be than the sign TWO WAY TRAFFIC, and although I would never advocate a blanket YIELD for all marital disagreements, the wisdom of GIVE WAY TO THE RIGHT is surely beyond question. So is DO NOT ENTER for anyone asked to take sides in the tiff. And for anyone contemplating some extra-marital dalliance, there is sternly unequivocal advice in WRONG WAY GO BACK!

Road signs remind us that some people, although they have hearts of gold, do have ROUGH EDGES. Others, when they go to the pub, are SUBJECT TO FLOODING. School children faced with Year 12 exams are warned it's a STEEP GRADE, and farmer's wives, when dressing for a day in the sheepyards, are reminded to SELECT LOW GEAR.

The saddest sign I saw in all my travels was ELDERLY CITIZENS CROSS HERE! I did hope they would be happy again further on. The most disappointing sign was 'P', which seldom provided the facilities I expected there to perform that function. The most poignant sign was SLOW CHILDREN, and the most misleading was that hilarious absurdity MEN AT WORK.

Altogether the signs on our roads not only safeguard our lives but enrich them as well, and everyone should make a point of noticing of them.

Especially my very favourite sign—CAUTION—DANGEROUS WHEN FROSTY!—because afterall, doesn't that apply to us all?

THE GREAT AUSTRALIAN SHOUT

After a hectic period of work on the farm, there's nothing better than to go into town, meet a friend at a favourite restaurant and have lunch together.

And when it comes time to pay . . .

THE GIRLS' LUNCH

THE MEN'S LUNCH

'Now, Jenny, lunch is on me.'

'Heavens, no! It's my shout today, Sue.'

'Don't be silly. I asked you to come, and I'm paying. I insist. Waiter! Could you bring me the bill, please?'

'Now listen, Sue. Put your money away. I'M paying for this lunch. It's my pleasure. And I must say it was delicious, wasn't it? Isn't it a treat to have something you haven't cooked yourself? What do you think they put in the *Matelote* sauce to give it such a tang?'

'A dash of cayenne, probably. Waiter! I'll have that bill over here, thank you!'

THE GIRLS' LUNCH   THE MEN'S LUNCH

'Look, stop it, Sue. You're causing a scene. Everyone is staring at us. Just give ME the bill and stop making a fuss. I'm so sorry about this, waiter. My friend here is very stubborn.'

'No, I will NOT give you the bill. It's my treat. I insist. You can take me next time.'

'That's what you said last time.'

'Nonsense, Jenny. You paid last time.'

'No, you did.'

'No, *you* did.'

'Look, this is ridiculous. Couldn't we go Dutch?'

'Absolutely not. Here we are, waiter. You can keep the change.'

'Well, thank you awfully, Sue. The lunch was delicious and I thoroughly enjoyed myself. But don't forget. Next time I'm taking you.'

'Well, we'll see . . .'

Lunch today is on me, Bob.'

'Oh, thanks, Bill.'

THE SINS OF SYNTAX

Although children at school are still taught the three R's—remedial reading, remedial writing and remedial 'rithmetic—it is my opinion (and I'm unanimous in this) that young people of today do not know how to write good English. They have learnt nothing about vocabulary or grammar. Some of them are apathetic about it, and the rest just can't be bothered.

Not like in my day. I grew up among that generation of school children who were lucky enough to be taught by rote and soundly drilled in syntax and grammar. For instance, we had it drummed into us from an early age that when you are describing something you should never use more than two adjectives running. Yet this is the kind of silly, sloppy, careless, uninformed, stupid, senseless and ignorant type of mistake you see everyday in young people's writing.

My generation of students was taught that to actually split an infinitive was a grammatical sin to assiduously avoid. We would never not recognise a double negative, and as for being found ignorant of the knowledge of the perfect infinitive, we should have died to have been.

I think parents concerned about the lax teaching methods of today should help their children to improve their standard of English themselves. I always guide my daughter in her homework. I encourage her to use correct parsing principles in sentence construction and to avoid using any one word repeatedly in the one sentence. The other night I corrected an exercise she had done for her teacher on the usage of the past participle 'had'. I, where my daughter had had 'had', had had 'had had'; 'had had' had had the approval of her teacher. Quite correct, I said, and notice also that that 'that' that that sentence contained should have been 'which'.

This careless modern attitude towards language use

has spawned a fresh crop of that ubiquitous grammatical mistake—the mixed metaphor. This is a deplorable error. It casts a shadow over the beauty of the English language. It is a snake in the grass—and we must nip it in the bud.

Another heinous etymological crime—tautology—is prevalent in the writing of the young. Perhaps this excessive, overdone use of two words which mean the same thing is just a passing phase, but children of today should stick to true facts about a proposed project, and it is vitally necessary to remember the old adage that the future lies ahead.

How lucky for my generation that our teachers instilled into us such a thorough knowledge of subjunctives and indefinites, passives and possessives. Not for us this careless modern writing where students can't even remember how to quote their childhood proverbs.

We shall never forget such stirring *bon mots* as 'a bird in the hand gathers no moss', and 'an apple a day and the pounds will look after themselves'. Or, as our biology teacher (there was no Human Relations Course nonsense in our day) used to tell us: 'People in glass houses shouldn't.'

Finally, which brings me to my last point, I think parents are quite justified in their concern, reflected so often in your pages, about the poor standard of English taught in schools today. Children should learn their language skills from the older generation. We studied grammar and syntax the old-fashioned way, and we know that a preposition is a word you should *never* end a sentence with.

BY THEIR MAILBOXES
ARE THEY KNOWN . . .

In the country, a mailbox is a symbol of great importance. It is the principal link of communication between the farm and the outside world.

Farm mailboxes come in all shapes and sizes: large and small, plain and fancy, old and new. I have always been intrigued by their great variety, and how much they reveal about their owners' individual personality and attitude to life.

For instance, down our road there is a mail receiver which is not so much a box as a house. It is at least three metres square, made of gleaming white weatherboard with a grey tiled roof.

Every time I drive past I wonder what on earth are the owners expecting in the mail that could possibly be that big—and need a seat to sit on to wait for it to arrive? Are they expecting woolpacks full of newsy letters from their friends? Or are they anticipating a container load of presents at Christmas time? Whatever the reason, I think that letterbox displays truly Great Expectations—a wonderfully optimistic outlook on life.

At the other extreme is the property whose mailbox comprises nothing more than a tiny tin cylinder, usually a bit of cast-off down-pipe, which seems to state that the only contact its owner ever expects to receive from the outside world is an occasional *Stock and Land*.

Between the two, of course, there is a great range of mailboxes, all displaying various degrees of imaginative diversity and all, whether intentionally or not, making a personal statement of some kind.

There are some, for example, which are strictly no-non-sense, practical and low-cost, like a cut-down plastic drench container sitting atop an old fence post. It is not hard to read the underlying message there. In dairying areas superceded cream cans are popular too, and say much the same thing.

Prevalent all over the country are old white-painted oil drums of various sizes—1, 4, or 12 gallon—depending on the optimism quotient of their owners. But even these embrace a wide range of styles. Some are mounted from the base and others are suspended. Some open inwards towards the homestead, and others open outwards towards the road. Some have tight-fitting lids and even locks attached. Others have a great gaping hole. Fascinating.

Some mailboxes have a beautifully routed wooden sign attached, proudly proclaiming the name of their home farm. Others are identified by a quick squirt of black paint over the woolpack stencil. Others again bear no form of identification at all, as if their owners are saying I-know-who-lives-here-and-it's-no-one-else's-bloody-business.

There is one delightfully original mailbox near us which I always enjoy as I drive past. It is a 4-gal drum painted a soft shade of pink, with a little metal snout and two pointy little metal ears attached to the front and a curly wire tail attached to the back. It's wonderfully lifelike, but to extract the mail you have to lift the tail and plunge your arm into the gaping hole beneath. I do not think I would find that aesthetically pleasing in the long term.

Occasionally I come across a wonderfully whimsical mailbox, which has for a stand a rigid chain or an old auger blade or even a single-furrow mulboard plough. I always enjoy the 'Look!-I-can-weld!' genre, too. These singular examples of contemporary art, usually abstract expressionist in theme, are concocted from an array of disused engine parts, scraps of fencing wire and RHS steel off-cuts all welded together to produce a piece of modern sculpture of which Alberto Giacometti would be proud.

By contrast, other mailboxes seem to make a point of being seriously natural—or is it naturally serious?—compromising an unpainted hollow log jammed into the fork of a cut-down gum tree.

There are still a number of old refrigerators around

serving as letterboxes—although what they say about their owners I daren't imagine. There is also the occasional converted woolpress, and even, not far from us, a huge old radial tank engine minus its crankshaft, mounted on a post.

Maybe after all this you are wondering what we ourselves use as a mailbox? Ours is a superannuated dog kennel—although what that reveals about us I'm not exactly sure.

Perhaps it implies that in regard to my theory of mailboxes, I am probably barking up the wrong tree.

OH, WHAT A TANGLED WEB WE WEAVE . . .

Do you know who said: 'Let us begin by committing ourselves to the truth; to see it like it is and tell it like it is; to find the truth, to speak the truth and to live the truth'? It was Richard Nixon.

I am concerned about the decline in basic honesty in society today. It seems to me that truth has become such a rare and precious commodity in the community that many people think it best used sparingly.

Politicians have the reputation for being the worst liars, but this is probably unfair. 'My Prime Minister is wedded to the truth,' a backbencher once told me. 'It's just that like all married couples, they do live apart from time to time.'

Fishermen are known as consummate liars, so I was pleasantly surprised recently upon asking my son how many fish he had caught, to be told: 'Well, when I catch this one I'm after, and two more—I'll have three.' Devious, maybe, but no lie.

People in the country have always had a reputation for honesty, but I wonder how justified it is? For instance, have you ever been guilty of inflating your rainfall just a teeny bit in order to say you had more than your neighbour? If three quarters of your crop is fantastic, but the last quarter has been ruined by waterlogging, do you ever eliminate the poor area from the average when you are quoting your yield? Do you always declare the skin money on your tax return?

I find the concept of truth and honesty a minefield to try to explain to children. After years of stressing how vital it is always to tell the truth, you reach a point where you must backtrack and explain that sometimes truth ('Grannie, your new hat looks ghastly!') can be cruel and hurtful and should be softened somewhat. Trouble is, with children the little white lie usually ends up a double feature in technicolor.

My husband is adept at treading the fine line between being honest and being kind. The other evening we attended a particularly dreary dinner party, and as we left he said to his hostess: 'Thank you so much, I've had a marvellous evening!' then mumbled in the car as we drove off: 'But this wasn't it.'

Some people are refreshingly honest about their age, but even this seemingly simple truth can cause problems. Of one woman who told the truth about her age, Saki wrote: 'She said she was 42 and five months. It may well have pleased the angels, but her elder sister was not gratified.'

The area in which most people crave total honesty is in their personal relationships. Yet from here come the most-told lies in life. 'I love you', and 'Of course there's no-one else,' and that now that new lie which is sweeping the world: 'Don't worry, it's only a cold sore.'

My own suspicion is that the decline in basic honesty parallels the demise of the conscience—that still, small voice which makes you feel still smaller. The only still, small voice many people hear today comes from their walkman headsets. I wonder if perhaps in society's concern to protect the younger generation from any psychological scars we may have suffered from going through agonies of guilt, we have gone too far the other way, and kids never get to Feel Awful anymore?

But shouldn't there be a happy medium—as a famous clairvoyant once said?

However, that honesty is always the best policy was bought home to me recently when I was in a butcher's shop one morning, waiting to be served. Ahead of me a little old lady was buying a leg of lamb. 'That's $7.80,' said the butcher as he weighed it on his scales.

'Too small, I'm afraid,' she said. 'Do you have a larger one?'

The butcher took the leg back to his coolroom at the rear of the shop, put it down, paused for a moment, then picked up the same one (it was obviously the last) and took it back out to his customer, saying chirpily: 'This one should do nicely. It's $9.20.'

I was about to explode in protest, when I noticed the little old lady give a sweet, deadly smile. 'Thank you,' she said. 'That's perfect. I'll have both.'

THE DIARY OF A VICTORIAN COUNTRY LADY

MONDAY: Up at sparrows, bright-eyed and bushy-tailed to help load sheep for market. Transport due at six. Ready and waiting in sheepyards at five to. Transport finally arrives at nine. Load sheep in stony silence. Spend what's left of morning baking cakes for church stall. Serve on church stall in local village from two till four. Then go on to Guide and Brownie LA meeting at school. Collect children from ballet lessons and tennis practice at five-thirty. After dinner attend Bush Nurse Committee meeting, bright-tailed and bushy-eyed.

TUESDAY: Off to town for lunch with The Gels! Up at the crack to prepare. Press dress, wash hair, dig the garden from under nails. At eleven 'im Outdoors roars in, red in the face, hair on end and covered in dust. Would I have time to help draft one tiny mob of ewes before I go? Two hours later slip away briefly to the telephone. Postpone town lunch till Thursday. Flystrike in the weaners. Spend the afternoon in sheepyards, jetting. After dinner attend meeting of swimming pool committee.

WEDNESDAY: My golf day! The sun shines, the birds sing and the fairways beckon! Practise my putting with vacuum cleaner head as I whizz through house. Change and load golf clubs into car. Telephone rings. Have I remembered I'm on school canteen duty from ten until two? Unload golf clubs from car. Grumpily. Home at two-thirty and spend rest of afternoon weeding in veg garden. At eight, Parents' Association at school.

THURSDAY: At last! Off to town to see my friends! Up at dawn to prepare. At eight, the sound of racking sobs. The boy has a sore throat. Goodbye lunch. The other children go off to school as usual. When school bus safely past front gate, the boy shows sudden marked improvement. By ten, he's in the pink. Chinese checkers (three games) draughts (four games) Uno (one game). Over lunch, 'im Outdoors announces that a red-gum limb has fallen over north boundary fence so if I've got nothing else to do this afternoon (Ha! ha!) could I possibly take over feeding the sheep with the ute and oat trailer while he fixes the fence? The boy comes along to open gates for me while I drive. By the second paddock I realise I'm opening the gates while HE drives.

FRIDAY: On duty serving in Red Cross Shop from ten till four, then race home to catch up on the week's baking and ironing. Find 'im Outdoors waiting for me in kitchen with sickly grin and sickly sheepdog. A grass seed-infected ear. If I'm not too busy (Ha! ha!) could I possibly pop straight into town (85 k's away) and take the dog to the vet? Arrive home about seven-thirty. Cubs and scouts meeting at eight.

SATURDAY: Working bee all morning in school grounds, chipping paths and weeding beds. Working bee all afternoon at home, chipping beds and weeding paths. At night, out to dinner with friends nearby. Stagger home at four in the morning.

SUNDAY (Day of Rest):   Up at first light to rake out the house, tidy, dust, do the flowers and cook the Sunday roast. At one, some friends bring their city cousins to lunch. We sit around the dining-table chatting till four. As I offer her more coffee, the city wife comments languidly: 'What a relaxed, carefree lifestyle you have in the country. How lovely to have so much spare time to yourself,' and as I pour her coffee I spill some on her sleeve. It was an accident. No, it wasn't.

CAVEAT EMPTOR

To a farmer's wife, a trip to town is a treat, a holiday, a longed-for Day Out. It's a chance to shed her androgynous country gear and dress up, browse through the shops at leisure, perhaps meet some friends at a restaurant for lunch, or peruse a gallery.

However, in my experience, what more usually happens is something like this:

'Darling, could you get me a couple of little things in town today?' called my husband as I was rushing out the door one morning last week. 'Just one or two. Won't take you a minute.'

I've heard that before, I sighed to myself as he handed me his list. And any second now he'll say he hates to be a bother, but it's really important.

'I hate to be a bother but it's really important,' he said. Then, zapping me with his most winning smile: 'And could you possibly go in the ute? It needs a service.'

When I finally bounced into town that day, hair on end and covered in dust, the weather was already rather hot and blustery.

So was I.

I drove the ute straight around to the garage and asked the foreman *please* to have it finished as soon as possible as I had a lot of jobs to do. I had a list of household shopping as long as my arm, plus appointments to keep, bills to pay, library books to change, dry cleaning to collect, a saddle to be mended, & c. And, as always, I had to be back home again in good time to meet the school bus.

'It'll be ready at noon, no worries!' said the mechanic, so, grabbing my basket out of the back, off I set on foot.

Firstly, I thought, I'll do the farm list. Get that out of the way. After all, my husband said it would only take a few minutes.

'Could I have a set of 4½" points for a spring release drill,' I asked the MF salesman when I reached the machinery dealer's.

'Sure. What kind of points? Knock-on or bolt on?'

I looked at the list. Of course it didn't say. Yet I knew that if I got it wrong, I'd be in the poo. 'Better take both,' I replied.

'Sorry, we've only got bolt-on. You'll have to go around to Freddie's in Thomson Street for the others.'

Off I trudged to Freddie's in Thomson Street. 'I can help you with half a set,' said Freddie when I arrived, hauling the points up on to the counter, black and clanking, in front of me. 'You'll probably get the rest down at Bert's in Bell Parade.'

Neither knock-on nor bolt-on steel points are light to carry. I acquired the remainder at Bert's in Bell Parade then staggered back to the garage, perspiring profusely.

'Might be a little later with the ute,' the mechanic told me as I dumped the points into the back. 'Found a slight problem with the carbie. I'll need another half hour.'

Inwardly groaning, off I went to the hardware store for the next little items on The List. Now we have a very good hardware store in our town. It has a wonderful range of merchandise offered to its customers through 'prompt, courteous, efficient *self-service.*'

With a feeling of rising panic I bustled up and down row after row of gleaming hardware—nuts, bolts, washers, screws, nails—in every possible shape and size, all done up in neat un-openable plastic packets and labelled in Chinese hieroglyphics. Meanwhile, time was ticking inexorably on. I looked around for help, but there was no staff to be seen. I should have known, I sighed, they're all Miltonists here. Miltonists are salesmen who believe 'they also serve who only stand and wait.'

Eventually I found one sipping coffee under his counter. 'Could I have some nails, please,' I said. 'About 250 g's. 2.8 cm.'

'Righto, love. What sort?'

'What do you mean "what sort?" 'Surely a nail is a nail is a nail!'

'Aw no, lady. You can have bullet head nails or flat head nails, roofing or flex sheet, wall board or . . . '

'Some of each,' I replied. 'And six bolts, please, 10 × 1 cm.'

'Engine or coach bolts?' asked the assistant. 'Cad plated or black? Spring washers or flat?'

'Some of each again, thank you,' I mumbled.

'Sorry, haven't go any cad-plated. Sold the last ones ten minutes ago. You'll have to pop around to Farm-mart in Grange Road for those.'

By this time the sun was beating down mercilessly. With a heavy parcel under each arm, I 'popped' around to Farm-mart in Grange Road, three blocks away, ac-quired the cad-plated bolts, then headed grimly for the stock agent's, next on The List. By now the morning had almost slipped away, and a large, wet blister had formed on my left heel.

'4 × 500 mls 6-in-1 sheep vaccine, please,' I said, smiling this time, for I could spy a whole pile of it in packets on the counter in front of me.

'Bring an Esky, did you, lady?' asked the salesman. 'Gotta have an Esky in this heat to keep it below 4 C.'

Back to the garage for the Esky which I had actually brought in for ice cream and other assorted frozen goodies. 'Funny thing,' said the salesman when I returned. 'Only seem to have 3 packets of 6-in-1 vac-cine here.'

'What about those?' I demanded imperiously, point-ing at the pile on the counter.

'Old stock. Past their Use By date. Can't sell you those. However, if you just nick around to Dalgety Farmer's in Auburn Street—I'm sure they'll fix you up.'

Lugging the half-full Esky, I 'nicked' around to Auburn Street two blocks on, bought the remainder of the vaccine, then headed back to the garage.

'Sorry, the ute won't be ready for a while yet. Got a problem with the back suspension.'

'So have I,' I murmured, and headed for the nearest public telephone. From there, with an increasing sense of *déjà vu,* I rang my friends and said to carry on lunch without me. Then I postponed my appointment with the dress-maker, cancelled my hairdo and rang a neighbour to ask her could she please collect the children off the school bus as I wouldn't be home in time?

After that I set out for the pasture seed supply depot, the next place on The List.

And when at the end of the day I eventually arrived home, head splitting and fewer than half my own chores done, my husband rushed out to greet me, and, beaming all over, said: 'Have a great time in town today, darling? Have a lovely Day Out?'

Frankly, I am not prepared to divulge my reply.

THE PERFECT GUEST

Once I saw a plaque inside someone's front door which read: 'If we get to drinking Sunday afternoon and start insisting you stay over until Tuesday, please remember we don't mean it.'

As Prince Phillip once said, the art of being a perfect guest is knowing when to leave. But to be a perfect guest you need other qualities as well, and it's ironic that these qualities are really only appreciated when they are lacking.

Recently we invited some friends up from the city to stay with us on our property for a long weekend, and we were thrilled when they said they could come. Dear friends whom we hadn't seen for at least five years, we awaited their visit with eager anticipation.

Five years is a long time. You can forget a lot in five years. We'd forgotten that they have four children, not three: two sons, a daughter—and a corgi.

We'd forgotten that the corgi, while he hated sheep dogs, loved live ducklings.

We'd forgotten that the elder son was an aspiring rally driver, winning pole position in a solo ciruit around the machinery shed in the farm ute, then roaring off to do some heavy circle work in and out amongst the lambing ewes.

We'd forgotten that to the younger son our garden paths made a perfect motorbike mini-Le Mans, until he wrapped the farm Honda around the birdbath at five o'clock in the morning.

I can't think how it escaped our notice that the Little Princess loved to steal matches and dart off lighting fires amongst the patches of dry grass not far from the (nearly full) hayshed.

With the passing of the years it had somehow slipped our memory that the parents never appeared for breakfast until we'd already completed hours of hard toil, then, wonderfully refreshed, delighted in keeping us up playing bridge and sipping port into the small hours—and wondering why our bidding was so distrait.

We'd certainly forgotten that each morning when the husband did finally appear he'd rub his hands together, and say: 'Well, now! What's on today? Golf? Tennis? Fishing?' when the weaners were due for a drench, the windmill had jammed, there was a wether bogged in the back creek and a limb had fallen over the fence between the ram paddock and the maiden ewes.

It's a wonder we never registered what a great compliment their children paid us by feeling so thoroughly at home in our house that they felt free to loot the biscuit cupboard and cake tins at will, so that each day all our arvos had disappeared by elevenses.

Somehow we'd forgotten from last time that the wife was a vegetarian who only ate special foods, like poly-unsaturated lettuce leaves and herbal tea. We'd forgotten also how, after each meal, she would stand by the sink gazing abstractedly at the mountain of dirty dishes, and saying: '*Do* tell me if there's anything I can do to help . . . '

Neither had we remembered that she had the city habit of putting Certain Things down the loo, thus blocking up the entire farm sewerage system for a week.

All in all, we'd forgotten how long a long weekend can be. But while there's an art in being a perfect guest, there's also an art in being a perfect host—and we admit we don't have it.

You see, we know a perfect host would never deliberately and mischievously send his guests out mushrooming—and forget to warn them about the electric fence.

MURDER IN THE CHOOKHOUSE

Doctors and sky-diving instructors may bury their failures, and architects plant vines, but when a farmer has a failure, she eats it!

I have had a terrible failure with chooks. I don't know why. I fed them conscientiously night and morning, changed their water, and regularly transferred their accumulated droppings to the lemon tree. But all to no avail. Under my careful and dedicated husbandry we had nine sleek, white, fat, happy *non-laying* hens.

I suppose the basic problem was that, though a lover of wild birds from way back, I really have no natural affinity for fowls. I am devoid of spiritual empathy for a chook. Even as a child The Little Red Hen always struck me as impossibly smug and self-righteous and I used to think Chicken Little and Henny Penny right twits.

So eventually, with feed bills mounting, a backyard of white feathers, a garden scratched into extinction and still *no eggs,* my husband said They Had To Go.

Mind you, I didn't give up easily. At feedtime as I cast the golden grain gently at their feet I would whisper to them softly and imploringly about our love of omelettes. But the nesting boxes stayed starkly empty.

One time I even sat on a stump outside the chookhouse with my guitar and sang to them Bob Dylan's lovely song 'Lay, lady, lay.' That did no good either.

At other times I tried assertiveness instead, hurling the grain at them stingingly, and shouting: 'Take that, ya little buggers, and *lay,* damm you, *lay!'*

On these occasions my husband called me fowlmouthed.

All in all, my achievement at poultry was paltry.

So eventually I asked a woman from our local town whom I knew to be a great success with chooks to take them away and 'dress' them for the deep freeze (a ridiculous expression when you think that actually it means the opposite).

She arrived at dawn, and together we prepared to storm their fortress. 'Murder in the chookhouse!' I cried, and, eyes clenched tightly shut, made a desperate lunge through the fowlhouse door. Feathers flew in all directions and shrieks and squawks rent the morning air. After five minutes of feathered mayhem I made a precarious purchase on the leg of one frantically flapping bird and looked around in triumph—to see my helper in calm and unruffled possession of all the rest.

She had one under each arm, another two held firmly by their feet, one more in her apron pocket and the last two somehow imprisoned beneath her ample bosom. It was a virtuoso performance. I stood there gazing in humble admiration. It is a moving experience to see anything in life Well Done.

A few minutes later all the chooks were bundled, still squawking, into three old wire possum traps on the back of her battered ute—and off she roared in a cloud of feathers, leaving me there to contemplate my failure and feel like a right old boiler myself.

Do chooks have souls, I wondered? On moonlit evenings will their ghosts come back to haunt me? Very likely, I suppose, because afterall, why did the chicken cross the road if not to get to The Other Side?

In the meantime, chicken maryland, *coq au vin, poulet Bretonne, Pollo en Mole*—failure in farming has delicious compensations.

MULGA JILL'S WINDSURFER

'Twas Mulga Jill, from Eaglemont, that caught the
windsurf craze;
She gave away the good old yacht that served her many
days;
She found a full-length wetsuit in a colour she adored,
Then hurried off to town and bought a shining new sail
board;
And as she put it on her car and attached it to the rail,
The grinning shop assistant said, 'Excuse me, can you
sail?'
'See here, young man!' said Mulga Jill, 'from Brighton
to the sea!
From Williamstown to Sandringham there's none can
sail like me!
I'm good all round at water sports, as everybody
knows,
I swim and surf and deep sea dive, and I love a wind
that blows!
For sailing is my special gift, my chiefest sole delight;
Just ask Phil Krakouer can he kick; Jeff Fenech can he
fight?

'Twas Mulga Jill from Eaglemont that went down to
the quay,
She launched the board, and raised the sail—then
headed out to sea;
She meant to hug the shore line right round by Hob-
son's Bay,
But 'ere she'd gone a dozen yards—it bolted clean
away!
It struck a wave, and gave a leap and cleared some
passing yachts!
It raced past a container ship doing easily thirty knots!

Across the gleaming water it shot from left to right!

While Jill, white-faced and terrified, clung fast with all her might!

Seaford, Frankston, Mornington—it screamed around the Bay!

Rosebud, Rye, Sorrento—it left them in its spray!

And finally as Mulga Jill was loosing her last grip,

An extra gust of wind came out and sent it out *The Rip*!!

'Twas Mulga Jill from Eaglemont, who slowly swam ashore,

She said: 'I've had some narrow shaves and lively rides before,

I've sailed single-handed to Tassie for a bet,

But this was *the* most awful ride that I've encountered yet.

I'll chuck that one-sailed outlaw; it's shaken all my nerve!

To feel it whistle through the air, and plunge and buck and swerve,

It's safe at rest beneath Bass Strait, we'll leave it lying still,

A reclining chair is good enough henceforth for Mulga Jill!'

AT THE BEACH . . .

There is a tide in the affairs of men, which, taken at the flood, almost reaches my toes. I am lying on a beach soaking in the sun and trying to keep track of my childrens' heads bobbing up and down before me in the bubbling brine. Trouble is, there are a million other soggy little heads out there as well and I am not certain that the three I am watching so assiduously are mine.

To the east and west of me, as far as the eye can see, the beach is crowded with reclining bodies, all in various states of dishabille, and all in dedicated pursuit of that hazardous but seemingly essential twentieth-century fashion accessory—le tan.

And from amongst this umber throng, I can pick a country family at a glance.

The country woman is the one with the suntan below the elbows only, and in a distinctive V at the neck. The country children are the ones with a suntan *all over*. And if the day is hot with a strong north wind, the country family is the one with the father is missing.

But today is cool and still, and the country father is there. He is the one lying on a beach towel dressed in bathers, socks and riding boots.

You only have burnt feet once.

I can pick a farming family, too, by the plethora of picnic baskets and hampers which surround them on the sand. This is not their lunch, mind you, merely arvo tea. No country person can survive more than two hours without food.

If I need still further clues, I look to their hats. Who else but a farmer wears a superannuated Akrubra to the beach—and keeps it on even in the water? Who else but a country child runs around quite happily in a peaked cap with *'Systamex Wipes Out Worms!'* printed on the front? Who else but a farmer's wife sports a colourful terry-towelling with *'Australian Artificial*

Breeders' emblazoned across it—and is quite oblivious to the curious looks of passersby¿

However, to make really certain, I search for the most distinctive feature of country people at the beach—the anxious, far-away look at the back of their eyes. This is because they never stop worrying about Things Back Home. Did he strain up the fence tightly enough to keep the steers out of the crop¿ Has a limb fallen and shorted out the electric fence¿ Will a possum get down the den chimney¿ Did he turn off the pump¿ Did she turn off the iron¿ *Did anyone turn off the deep freeze¿¿¿*

How come I am so sure about all these things¿ As someone once said: it takes one to know one. So when you're next at the beach and you see a family just like the one above, come on up and say hello. Slap us on the back. Ask us how we're peeling.

TO PART IS TO DIE A LITTLE . . .

There is an art in saying goodbye. Partings account for some of our most intense moments in life and should be handled with poise and *élan*. However, I think modern modes of farewell preclude this. The prosaic drabness of today's language has stifled the elegant exits of the past. 'Sweets to the sweet, farewell!' is now 'See ya'.

Lovers partings are always poignant, but they no longer seem poetic. Which would you rather have to treasure in your memory, to hug to yourself and re-live in a thousand lonely re-enactments—Austin's 'Now, in the summit of love's topmost peak, kiss and we part . . . ' or Bogart's 'Here's lookin' at you, kid'?

I believe the time has come to restore the graceful goodbyes of the past. Afterall, we restore old buildings of beauty and historical significance—why not farewells? I am starting a campaign to resurrect the poetic parting, and here are some suggestions from historical drama, literature and film: 'A fond kiss, and then we sever . . . ' is a good one. 'Thou art gone from my gaze like a beautiful dream!' is another. 'Lips to lips! Yet once more 'ere we part, clasp me and make me thine as mine thou art'. Isn't that more euphonious than 'Taa taa for now now'?

Then there is Emerson's 'Goodbye, proud world, I'm going home . . . ' and Shakespeare's Othello's 'Farewell the tranquil mind, farewell content!' or his own 'Let us not be dainty of leave-taking, but shift away', which I suppose is the Elizabethan equivalent of 'Don't call us, we'll call you'.

Of course many of these farewells lines come from scenes of high passion, the (one hopes) rare moments when life is rent by cataclysmic loss. However, if my campaign is to get off the ground, we need to use them in everyday situations.

So tomorrow morning when your beloved heads off out into the paddocks, instead of the usual rushed 'Bye, dear,' why not run to him with arms outstretched and cry: 'Partir, c'est mourir un peu!' Then that night, before drifting off to sleep whisper 'Goodnight, sweet prince. May flights of angels sing thee to thy rest'. For the next morning I suggest 'Adieu, my awin sweet thing, my joy and comforting', and so on.

A goodbye is a marvellous weapon of psychological warfare. If you can stage-manage a scene to create rising tension and emotion and then at its climax declaim a great parting line and sweep out, the effect will be devastating. Whatever impression you wish to convey, be it of anger, passion or remorse, a dramatic exit line will leave it lingering on in the room, like perfume, long after you have gone.

But for goodness sake do not leave anything behind after you when you flounce out. You will look awfully silly creeping back five minutes later to collect your cardigan.

Eloquent goodbyes can enrich our lives in many ways, and it is possible to extract poetry and pathos from even mundane chores. For instance, next time you leave for home after serving your turn on the local school canteen, try Lord Nelson's last words 'Thank God I have done my duty'. If one night your partner wishes to retire early but you still have some jobs to do around the house, how about 'The bed is lovely, dark and deep, but I have promises to keep, and the ironing to do before I sleep'?

On those occasions when he is a bit slow helping with the washing-up, do not nag, just quote Edward VIII's Abdication Speech: 'You must believe me when I tell you that I find it impossible to carry the heavy burden of responsibility and to discharge my duties as I would wish, without the help of the one I love ... ' then see if the tea-towel flies.

But let me issue a warning—don't overdo it. I was ignominiously check-mated recently and I do not want that to happen to you. Dashing up to the woolshed one evening to collect the crutchers' smoko basket, and not wishing to miss an opportunity for a dramatic exit, I called to my husband as I left: 'It is a far, far greater thing I do than I have ever done! It is a far, far better place I go to than I have ever known!'

He looked at me for a moment in exasperation, then gave a slow Rhett Butler smile and said: 'Frankly, my dear, I don't give a damn . . . '

WHERE SHEEP MAY SAFELY GAZE . . .

It has often been said that people are just like sheep. But for me the opposite also is true. I think sheep are just like people—in all their rich and varied individuality.

At least that's what's running through my mind as I'm trying to coax, cajole, bully and/or force 300 ewes into the race for a pre-lambing drench.

Standing in a cloud of dust with the mob circling around me I am struck again with the thought of how *human* some of the sheep seem, how *familiar*. They exhibit all the same personality types, body language and behavior patterns as people.

For instance, I notice a shy and timid little ewe who, quite unable to cope with responsibility, constantly rushes back to the rear of the mob, hiding her head, and trying to make herself as inconspicuous as possible.

Next my attention is caught by a big, fierce old girl with cascading woolly double-chins, who won't be hurried, can't be frightened, and who, after neutralising the sheepdog by eye-contact alone, rounds on me and stamps her foot in the dust.

The ewe behind her is all show and bravado, shaking her head to attract attention then making a rush towards the neck of the race with half the mob following along behind in admiration, but losing her nerve at the last moment, propping in a cloud of dust, then disappearing round the back to hide until she has plucked up enough courage to make another run later on.

Near the end of the mob I notice The Scream. Every group has one. The Scream is a fluffy little ewe who flounces about the yard shaking her ears, waggling her hips, showing off to her friends and constantly playing the clown.

What shapes a sheep's personality, I wonder, as I

push the Scream and her friends towards the mouth of the race? Is early experience of life the moulding factor—as it is with people?

For instance, is the shy, timid little ewe's poor social skills and chronically low level of self-esteem perhaps the result of a deprived and unhappy lambhood?

And did the fierce old ewe develop her aggressive attitude and exaggerated assertiveness from a dominating role-model in her youth, which she now feels the need to emulate?

The would-be leader's behavior demonstrates a deep sense of insecurity about her status in the social hierachy of the existing mob dynamics. What she needs is some reality therapy for the reformulation of her own self-concept—('am I a worthwhile sheep?' &c.) Perhaps she suffered maternal deprivation during early ruminant pubescence and never learned the strategies necessary for the setting of personal goals?

On the other hand, the behavior of The Scream is probably psychosexual in origin, I opine, the result of failure to resolve latent Oedipal problems during lambhood. Her aggressively attention-seeking behaviour is highly stress-related, and even suggests a history of possible lamb abuse.

As I shoo the last of the stragglers foward my musings are interrupted by the sudden sharp thought that if sheep really are like people—one of them must be like me! And—*which one?*

I shut the gate, call the dog to heel, and head off homeward with the distinctly uneasy suspicion at the back of my mind that, in any mob of sheep, I'm probably the black one . . .

NO WORRIES, MATE!

As someone once said, worries are like babies. The more you nurse them, the bigger they grow.

Farmers in Australia are besieged by worries at the moment, and one of my worries is how many worries can a person handle at the one time? Just how many anxieties can you service concurrently? I am finding it extemely difficult to do justice to all the worries I have right now—and that worries me.

First of all I have my great and grand worries like The Bomb and starvation and third-world debt; acid rain, apartheid, and Soviet expansionism. Next I have my national worries like our balance of payments problems, the fall of the dollar and deficit budgeting; unemployed youth, media monopolies and uranium mining in Kakadon't.

After that come my farming worries like drought and fire and fly-strike; take-all and stripe-rust and salt. Not to mention soaring costs and crashing prices, over-production and under-demand.

Meanwhile at home I have my family worries, like puberty and pimples, drugs and drink; exams and exhaustion, money and manners.

Then, at the end of the day, I still have my own personal little worries to worry about, like obesity and wrinkles, integrity and health.

And one of my biggest worries is that as I become older it's the little worries which worry me more than the big ones. Years ago when I was young I spent whole days worrying about Communist insurgency in south-east Asia or over-population in outer Mongolia; the oil cartel in the Middle-east or human rights in Argentina. But now I am old and world-weary I seem to spend more time worrying about the aphids on the roses and the mildew on the bathroom walls than the greenhouse effect on the ozone layer or the melting of the ice caps. And that worries me.

It's all too much. I can't cope. I simply can't do justice to all these worries at the one time. I've got agony-overload. So I've decided there's only one solution to all this worrying, and that is to *give it up*! Some people give up smoking or booze or chocolates. I'm giving up worrying.

After all, as a famous lift-driver once said, life has its ups and downs. Farmers have had problems before. Australia has had problems before. *The world* has had problems before. Getting ulcers over it won't make the slightest bit of difference.

So no more Agony Overload. No more eating my heart out. Not for nothing was coined that good old Aussie expression: 'No worries, mate!' And from now on, whenever anyone says it to me, I'm going to obey.

REQUIEM FOR A LETTER

Anyone who ever has awaited a love letter (and I hope everyone has) will recognise novelist Edith Wharton's description of its arrival: 'The first glance to see how many pages, the second to see how it ends, the breathless first reading, the slow lingering over each phrase, and finally the choosing of the one that will be carried in one's thoughts all day, making an exquisite accompaniment to the dull prose of life.'

Can a telephone call give you that?

I am concerned that the telephone is replacing the letter. Letter-writing, as a means of exploring a relationship at a distance, is going out of style.

I've reached this conclusion after making extensive inquiries in both city and country areas, and everywhere receiving the same response: yes, people now (whether lovers, family or friends) ring more often than they write, especially the young.

'I never have *time* to write', was the usual comment. 'Too busy. Too tired. The telephone is so much quicker and easier.'

Trouble is, it's also fearfully transient. Imagine the loss to the world if Elizabeth Barrett had felt too tired to write to Robert Browning, if Katherine Mansfield had been too busy to write to John Middleton Murry, and Zelda had always 'phoned Scott?

What a colourless portrait of their marriage would remain if Vita Sackville West had felt too busy or too tired to write to her Harold and had called him up instead each day they were apart.

Consider the consequences if the telephone had been available in Biblical times. 'Hello? It's Paul speaking. Paul the Apostle. Is that the Corinthians? Good. Now listen carefully because I'm too busy and too tired to write. "Love suffereth long and is kind." Yes, that's right. "K-i-n-d, KIND." Can you hear me? "Love vaunteth not itself, is not puffed up . . . "

I know it takes more time and effort to write a letter than to ring, but I believe the pleasure it bestows increases proportionately. 'My son used to write each week,' one mother told me, 'but now he always rings. I love to hear his voice, but the call is over so quickly, and I'm left feeling empty. His letters I used to read and reread for days.'

Some people told me they use the telephone only because they find it agonisingly difficult to express themselves on paper. 'I agree letters are more satisfying,' one girl said, 'but the moment I pick up a pen and face that blank sheet of paper, my mind freezes.'

Others are dissuaded from writing by caution. In this age of disposable handkerchiefs, disposable cups and disposable relationships, a letter *lasts*. There is future accountability inherent in committing thoughts to paper, and this frightens people. A telephone call is safer. It can always be forgotten or denied.

However, the telephone is not the only way of avoiding letter-writing. Stationers all around the country carry an astonishing array of printed greeting cards. Birth celebration cards, death condolence cards—and one for every possible occasion in life between. Happy Christmas/birthday/anniversary/voyage/homecoming; get well/thin/fit/rich/sober; congratulations upon graduation/promotion/marriage/divorce/vasectomy . . . Whatever message you wish to convey to someone there will be a card which says it for you. The only effort required is to sign your name.

Post cards too are abundant, their glossy photographs relieving the traveller of any need for descriptions.

I think these are a communication cop-out. Can you imagine George Bernard Shaw sending printed greetings to Ellen Terry? Would Abelard have been comforted by a Get Well card from Heloise? Would Josephine have melted to receive a postcard from Napoleon: 'Greetings from Austerlitz: Having lovely time—wish you were here'?

It would be sad indeed if the art of letter-writing

were to fade away. Nothing matches the joy of seeing familiar hand-writing on a bulging envelope.

But it does seem increasingly difficult to find the time to put pen to paper. And, to be honest, despite all good intentions, the only time I myself drop a line nowadays is when I am fishing.

I LOVE A SUNBURNT TORSO

The love of city polish,
Of manners most urbane,
Of clean, pink hands and faces,
Is running in some veins,
Strong love of suit and waistcoast,
White shirts and soft silk ties,
I know—but cannot share it,
My love is otherwise . . .

I love a sunburnt torso,
A chest of sweeping planes!
A man with rugged features,
And the country in his veins!
I love his skin-barked knuckles,
I love his knobbly knees;
His beauty and his terror—
It's a wide, brown man for me!

Core of my heart, my farmer!
With mud stains on his socks,
Sump oil on his moleskins,
Grass seeds in his jocks.
His pockets stuffed with hayband,
His boots caked in manure;
His constant smell of woolshed
For me holds great allure.

A tender-hearted tyrant!
A wilful, stubborn man!
All you who have not loved one—
You will not understand.
Though Earth holds many splendors,
Wherever I may lie,
I know to what brown torso
My homing thoughts will fly!

With abject apologies
to Dorothea Mackellar